Forensic Psychiatry for Health Professionals

This book is due for return not later than the last
date stamped below, unless recalled sooner.

THERAPY IN PRACTICE SERIES

Edited by Jo Campling

This series of books is aimed at 'therapists' concerned with rehabilitation in a very broad sense. The intended audience particularly includes occupational therapists, physiotherapists and speech therapists, but many titles will also be of interest to nurses, psychologists, medical staff, social workers, teachers or voluntary workers. Some volumes are interdisciplinary, others are aimed at one particular profession. All titles will be comprehensive but concise, and practical but with due reference to relevant theory and evidence. They are not research monographs but focus on professional practice, and will be of value to both students and qualified personnel.

FORTHCOMING TITLES

Forensic Psychiatry for Health Professionals

Chris Lloyd

Senior Occupational Therapist,
A.I.M.H.S., Gold Coast Hospital,
Queensland, Australia

CHAPMAN & HALL

London · Glasgow · Weinheim · New York · Tokyo · Melbourne · Madras

**Published by Chapman & Hall, 2–6 Boundary Row,
London SE1 8HN, UK**

Chapman & Hall, 2–6 Boundary Row, London SE1 8HN, UK

Blackie Academic & Professional, Wester Cleddens Road,
Bishopbriggs, Glasgow G64 2NZ, UK

Chapman & Hall GmbH, Pappelallee 3, 69469 Weinheim, Germany

Chapman & Hall USA, One Penn Plaza, 41st Floor, New York
NY 10119, USA

Chapman & Hall Japan, ITP-Japan, Kyowa Building, 3F, 2-2-1
Hirakawacho, Chiyoda-ku, Tokyo 102, Japan

Chapman & Hall Australia, Thomas Nelson Australia, 102 Dodds
Street, South Melbourne, Victoria 3205, Australia

Chapman & Hall India, R. Seshadri, 32 Second Main Road, CIT East,
Madras 600 035, India

Distributed in the USA and Canada by Singular Publishing Group Inc.,
4284 41st Street, San Diego, California 92105

First edition 1995

© 1995 Chapman & Hall

Typeset in 10/12pt Palatino by Mews Photosetting, Beckenham, Kent
Printed in Great Britain by Page Bros (Norwich) Ltd

ISBN 0 412 48350 5   1 56593 183 1 (USA)

A catalogue record for this book is available from the British Library

Library of Congress Catalog Card Number: 94-72650

∞ Printed on permanent acid-free text paper, manufactured in
accordance with ANSI/NISO Z39.48–1992 and ANSI/NISO
Z39.48–1984 (Permanence of Paper).

To Joan Lloyd and Merran Fiqia

Contents

Preface

Forensic psychiatry is a specialty area of practice that is developing rapidly. It involves the intermix of psychiatry and the law and is a relatively new area of practice for health professionals. The last decade has seen a change of focus in how to treat the mentally ill offender.

In the criminal justice process, forensic psychiatry deals with destructive, aggressive, and socially unacceptable behaviour. Both the criminal justice system and forensic psychiatry are concerned with encouraging the individual to exercise self control, with fostering individual change in behaviour, and protecting others members of society and property.

Recently there has been an increasing involvement of mental health professionals in both the assessment and treatment of forensic psychiatric clients. Health professionals who are currently employed in forensic settings have had to develop their role and formulate programmes to meet the complex needs of the forensic client population with relatively little published in the literature to guide them. Since forensic psychiatry is a new and developing field there exists the opportunity for health professionals to develop a significant role in the rehabilitation and reintegration of the forensic client into society.

With this being the case, there is a need to provide health professionals with a comprehensive book on the nature of the forensic system (from both the legal aspects and the impact it has on individuals), the types of clients seen, and ways in which treatment programmes can be planned and organized. By providing such a book, health professionals either working in the field or considering forensic psychiatry as a career choice will be better equipped to know how to treat a client whose psychiatric condition must be considered as well as the legal framework.

Specifically the aims of this book are:

1. To acquaint health professionals with the current status of forensic psychiatry.
2. To elaborate upon the type of setting that the health professional may be called upon to work in.
3. To highlight the client population that the therapist may come in contact with, including special needs minority groups.
4. To examine the impact that the environment has on the individual and how this influences the setting up of therapy programmes.
5. To look at the need for competent assessment in order to contribute to effective recommendations and treatment planning.
6. To present a number of therapy options that the health professional may consider employing when establishing a treatment programme; this includes outlining what types of media and techniques may be effective.

Since there is a lack of literature on the subject of health professionals and their role in forensic psychiatry, this book has the potential to be used as a resource material for both students and health professionals. These could include students with an interest in studying criminology and rehabilitative practices as well as a variety of health professionals such as occupational therapists, nurses, recreation officers, welfare officers, and social workers whose principal concern is this group of clients.

Acknowledgements

Many people are involved in the formulation of knowledge in a specialized area and in the providing of information and assistance in preparing a book. I would like to thank the following people for the time that we shared in forensic psychiatry, for the support, the interest, and the encouragement to try new ideas – the late Dr Roy Dry, Dr Richard Rockstro, Dr Oto Cadsky, Dr Lea Studer, Dr Ruben Lang, Nasir Fiqia, Heath Nightingale, Linda Cargill, Antoinette Alleyne, Steve Hogan, Tom Gorman and the late Mary Rowbotham. And in addition, I would like to thank Dr Frikkie Maas for the amount of time and work we have put in the area of client-centred therapy. I would also like to thank the following people for helping me gain new insights into the practice of group psychotherapy – Dr Andrew Frukacz, Dr Harvey Marable, and Nadia Zanco. I would like to thank the following people for sharing information about their forensic psychiatric programmes – Sarah Johnson, Head of Paramedical Services, Trent Regional Forensic Service, Arnold Lodge, Cordelia Close, Leicester, England; Wendy Becker, Chief Occupational Therapist, Otago Area, Health Board, Community Health Services, Dunedin, New Zealand; Samson Tse, Lecturer, Otago Polytechnic, Dunedin, New Zealand; Karen McElroy, Occupational Therapist, Commonwealth of Pennsylvania, Department of Public Welfare, Norristown State Hospital, Norristown, Pennsylvania, USA; Mel Harris, Occupational Therapist in Charge, Graylands Hospital, Claremont, Western Australia. Rex Maddock has given invaluable assistance in literature search and in providing new directions for thought. I would like to thank Joan Lloyd for all the time she spent doing literature search and general assistance in the organization of the manuscript. I would also like to thank Rosemary Morris, Senior Editor, Health Sciences, Chapman & Hall, Catherine Walker and Lisa Fraley, Editors, Chapman & Hall and Jo Campling, Series Editor, Health Sciences, Chapman & Hall for their patience and support while working through the process of producing the completed manuscript.

1

Forensic psychiatry

INTRODUCTION

Forensic psychiatry deals with psychiatric illness and criminality. Over the last number of years there has been a changing focus from that of predominantly punitive and security minded to that of rehabilitative. An increasing involvement of health professionals in forensic psychiatry has been taking place. The role and scope of what these health professionals are able to offer in forensic psychiatry has been starting to emerge. This is determined by opportunity, availability of resources, funding, level of security, and requirements of the legal system. This may vary greatly not only within a country but internationally.

This chapter aims to acquaint the health professional with the background to the development of forensic psychiatric services and with some of the changes that have been taking place in the delivery of service. This chapter explores:

- historical background
- forensic psychiatry
- education
- role of health professionals
- aspects of service delivery
- future directions.

HISTORICAL BACKGROUND

In a number of countries around the world there has been ongoing debate concerning mentally ill persons. The debate has centred around a number of issues: where to house mentally ill people? how to treat them? the level of security required? how best to protect society? what are the rights of mentally ill people? This has meant that there has been a complex interplay between a number of opposing forces: political, legal, medical and humanitarian.

Many changes regarding attitudes to the mentally ill and their care and treatment have taken place. The rate of change very much depended upon the prevailing social and political attitudes of the time (O'Brien and Branson, 1990).

The original mental hospitals were known as lunatic asylums whose patient populations consisted entirely of involuntary patients. Initially, there was little differentiation made between people having a mental illness and those people with mental illness who had committed a crime. If it was thought that the person's actions and behaviours warranted committal this then was the course of action taken. In due course in some countries such as England and Wales (Bluglass, 1981), Canada (Arboleda-Florez, 1981), and New Zealand (Rolle, 1992) special hospitals were established to provide special security conditions for those persons having dangerous, violent, or criminal behaviour.

Lunatic asylums were set up in the countryside, often in isolated rural locations and usually quite remote from where the person originated. People understood very little about mental illness and tended to fear those who were seen as being mad.

The asylums operated as an independent community. They were closed to the outside world, usually surrounded by high walls with locked doors and barred windows. They tended to grow produce on their own farms and gardens and so on the whole were self-sufficient. This limited the contact with people in the local community (Bluglass, 1990).

Staff in these asylums were not trained in the management of mental illness; their role was that of custodian. Staff and patients alike shared chores and responsibilities for their mutual well-being. The medical superintendent had total power over what took place within the asylum (Bluglass, 1990).

Very little was known about the aetiology of mental illness and what could be done to treat the symptoms. Consequently, whatever illness had caused the person to be detained in the first place was unlikely to improve and it was rare for people to leave the asylum and return to their own community.

By the twentieth century, new trends and treatment options were becoming evident in the care of the mentally ill. Theories such as psychoanalysis and behaviourism were developing and new treatment methods were being tried, for example, milieu therapy, activities, industrial therapy and electric and insulin shock therapies. Staff were beginning to be trained in treatment methods for the mentally ill.

It was not until the 1950s, however, that radical changes started taking place in mental hospitals. The introduction of psychopharmacology and tranquillizers changed the face of mental health care. Now it became possible to reduce many of the gross pathological symptoms and acting-out behaviours which had formerly interfered with treatment. Psychiatric hospitals became less custodial and more therapeutic places.

Social psychiatrists began exploring new avenues, for example, Maxwell Jones (1953) promoted the idea of the therapeutic community handling the problem of mental illness. Psychologists such as Carl Rogers (1951) advocated a client-centred approach in working with clients seen in therapy situations.

Legislation regarding mental health clients changed in a number of countries around the world and procedures for admission to, detention in, and discharge from hospitals were established. The growth of the civil rights movement promoted looking at more safeguards for the rights of committed clients. Other changes that have taken place include the increased emphasis on the therapeutic milieu, increased numbers of voluntary clients, far fewer committed clients, open-door policies, half-way houses, family services, day-hospitals, community centres, closure of large psychiatric facilities, the building of smaller purpose built clinics and increased numbers of trained and qualified health professionals.

With all the changes taking place in general psychiatry, there has been an increasing awareness of the need to provide proper treatment facilities and options for the mentally abnormal offender, whether in prison, hospital or in the community (Bluglass, 1981). Psychiatric units became increasingly reluctant to admit clients who were difficult and dangerous (Snowden, 1985). It also became evident that, since deinstitutionalization, the prisons were holding an increasing number of persons with a mental illness (Reeder and Meldman, 1991; Stein and Diamond, 1985).

In a number of countries around the world, working parties or special committees were set up to look at the issue of mentally abnormal offenders and their disposition. Various recommendations were suggested such as the establishment of the regional secure unit programme in Britain (Snowden, 1985) and the regional forensic psychiatric services in New Zealand (Chaplow, 1992).

FORENSIC PSYCHIATRY

Forensic psychiatry has developed on a broad base as a recognized specialty within psychiatry in only a short number of years (Taylor, 1988). In almost every country of the world there is increasing interest in the subject (Gunn, 1986). The distinguishing feature of forensic psychiatry is the close relationship that exists between the legal process and the mentally abnormal offender. According to Gunn (1986), the expansion of interest in forensic psychiatry is related to:

- a complex series of social pressures;
- new assessment and treatment skills;
- increasing interest in what takes place in institutions;
- rising concern with the prediction of dangerousness; and
- increasing demands from a range of social institutions, notably the courts.

Forensic psychiatrists tend to focus on the management and treatment of the mentally abnormal offender, psychiatric legal issues, preventative measures, assessing particular problems such as the level of dangerousness and psychiatric ethics (Bluglass, 1981). In some countries such as Britain the emphasis has been on institutions and the management and treatment of mentally abnormal offenders (Bluglass, 1981). In other countries such as Australia forensic psychiatry is predominantly based in private practice and is quite underdeveloped with respect to the provision of adequate forensic psychiatric services even in the major cities (O'Brien and Branson, 1990). Whereas in the USA, forensic psychiatrists tend to confine their role to arguing cases through the courts and rarely treating patients (Taylor, 1988).

There are a number of differing categories of forensic psychiatric patients; in general these will include:

- persons who are unfit to plead or to stand trial;
- persons found fit to stand trial but subsequently found to be mentally ill;
- persons who have been held fully responsible for their crimes but became mentally ill during their confinement; and
- persons being assessed for a court report.

Mentally abnormal offenders may be detained in a variety of ways: general psychiatric hospitals, maximum security hospitals, hospital units within a prison complex, prisons, and special units or locked wards within the precincts of psychiatric hospitals. An alternative way of dealing with people who have committed an offence and who are suffering from a mental illness, depending on the category of the offender, the treatment needs, and community services is on an outpatient basis under a probation order that specifies treatment.

Working with the mentally abnormal offender requires a co-operative team approach that takes into account the specific needs of the individual, the family, and psycho-social and environmental issues. Mentally abnormal offenders are a complex client group, not only because of their illness and criminal behaviour, but because of the effects of their environment and ongoing legal constraints. Also, another significant difference in working with mentally abnormal offenders, as compared with a general psychiatric population, is that a large number of staff and different agencies, for example, probation, social and community services tend to be involved with each person (Gunn and Taylor, 1983).

There is a challenge in developing programmes and acquiring expertise in providing adequate management of clients who may be dangerous, violent, and have criminal behaviour coupled with mental illness. According to Gunn and Taylor (1983), although many of the general principles of rehabilitation apply in working with this client group, there are a number of additional factors to consider. These include:

- concentrating on an improvement in lifestyle rather than aiming for a return to a pre-morbid level of function;
- taking into account the number of secondary problems that individuals will have resulting from time spent in closed and authoritarian institutions;
- understanding how the dual stigma of mental illness plus criminal behaviour will have an effect on efforts to reintegrate the person into society;
- recognizing that offender-patients generally exhibit chronicity, usually have very low self-esteem, often exhibit learned negative behaviour; and
- ensuring there is continued involvement in the legal process.

EDUCATION

With the advent of forensic psychiatry as a specialty within psychiatry and the establishment of new forensic services has come the need for increased staffing levels and the need for a multidisciplinary approach to treatment. There have been difficulties in both attracting and then in keeping staff for a number of reasons: it is a relatively new area of practice and there is a limited amount of resource material available; there is confusion over roles and staff conflict and it is an area where there is perceived stress, tension, and violence (Snowden, 1985).

A key issue has been that few staff entering into forensic psychiatry had received training or education specific to forensic psychiatry or had experience working in this area. Bluglass (1981) emphasized the need to improve programmes of training in forensic psychiatry. Gunn (1986) felt that there was a neglect in university education to provide training in forensic psychiatry. Educational advantages include the building of a distinct body of knowledge on which to base practice, increased skill and confidence in treatment delivery and research expertise.

With the recognition that education in the area of forensic psychiatry is advantageous in the effective delivery of service, a number of changes have taken place, although not as rapidly as had been hoped. A review of the literature indicates some of the areas that have been explored. In Britain, for example, university chairs in forensic psychiatry have been set up and there is an expectation that medical personnel should receive some grounding in the care and management of the mentally abnormal offender. In Canada there are a number of clinics and treatment facilities that are affiliated with universities. Education for various professionals in forensic psychiatry is provided and research in forensic psychiatry is promoted (Bradford, 1990).

In a number of Australian universities nursing and allied health care professionals can take an elective course in forensic psychiatry and undertake a practicum in one of the forensic facilities (Lloyd, 1994). A number of American universities offer a post-graduate certificate in forensic nursing and a master's degree in forensic nursing for nurses who would like to add forensic nursing to their expertise (Birk, 1992).

Rossenrode and Cottingham (1992) describe the development of a graduate certificate course in forensic psychiatry for nurses working in the New Zealand forensic psychiatric system. The emphasis in this course was on increasing skills in the clinical setting, providing accountable and effective health care in the forensic setting, and establishing a wide number of resource persons to further assist their skills acquisition.

Platt *et al.* (1977) describe an occupational therapy field placement at a US federal correctional institution. The aim of this programme was for students to experience how occupational therapy can function in a non-medical setting.

It is hoped that this developing trend in academic forensic psychiatry will continue to gain momentum. It is only by initiating developments in education, research and resources that better provision of care will be provided to this traditionally neglected client group.

ROLE OF HEALTH PROFESSIONALS

People working in forensic psychiatry bring with them their basic training and the core skills of their profession. Then, depending upon the setting and the needs of the patients, a wide variety of roles have been developed in forensic psychiatry. A review of the literature reveals that a number of different health professionals – nurses, social workers, physiotherapists, occupational therapists, psychologists, and therapeutic recreators – have been defining their role.

Cook (1991) describes the interesting development of the role of the community psychiatric nurse and the court, where the nurses visit people who have been charged with an offence to determine whether or not they have a mental illness. The aim of this programme is to prevent people with a mental illness being caught up in the criminal justice system instead of receiving psychiatric care.

It has been found that mentally abnormal offenders living in the community require a high level of support and supervision. Forensic community psychiatric nurses are involved with the probation services, court diversion schemes and referrals for assessment and designing care plans for individual clients in the community. Owing to the diverse needs of forensic clients they take an eclectic approach in nursing intervention (Chaloner and Kinsella, 1992).

When forensic nurses were asked to rank competencies in terms of their usual work situation in order of importance, the following were rated highly: communicate effectively, maintain security, perform the nursing process and maintain the nursing role (Niskala, 1986).

Burrow (1991) describes the difficulties experienced by special hospital nurses who must maintain security while simultaneously creating therapeutic relationships with their patients. Nurses in these settings may take part in ward searches, body searches and escort duty – taking the patient to workshops, recreational facilities and so on. A major part of the special hospital nurses' role centres on control. However, despite these difficulties, the special hospital nurses have been involved in initiatives to improve their clients' prospects for a well-integrated life in the community, for example, taking their patients for shopping and family visits (Burrow, 1991) and in establishing family therapy projects so that families can become directly involved with their relative while in the special hospital (McCann, 1991).

Reeder and Meldman (1991) stress the need for nurses working in the prison system to have a strong foundation in crisis intervention and to provide short-term supportive therapy for the mentally ill offender. They suggest utilizing a biopsychosocial model of practice to further the development of theory and programmes for this group of clients.

A very different nursing role is described by Lynch (1991) who looks at the forensic clinical nurse specialist in the emergency department. There are a number of contributions that the forensic clinical nurse specialist can make to forensic science, for example, retaining evidence, liaison role to law enforcement and trauma victims' and expert witness testimony.

Key areas of concern for offenders leaving prison are accommodation, employment and money or benefits. Social workers play a major role in assisting prisoners in these areas. Prisoners need a wide range of facilities and services to support them on release, and the prison-based social worker acts as a liaison with colleagues in the community to arrange these supports (Hinton, 1976). Corden and Clifton (1985) discuss the need for the provision of after-care for socially isolated prisoners once they are released from prison. They stress the need for awareness of this group of prisoners and the need to provide services since this group of people usually encounter immediate and urgent problems on release.

Health problems seen by physiotherapists in prisons include high impact trauma, general musculoskeletal disorders, and respiratory and neurological conditions. The physiotherapist is involved in providing short-term rehabilitation and education (Goyert, 1991).

The occupational therapist is concerned about the individual's capability to carry out required tasks and roles in the areas of self-care, work, and leisure. Jones and McColl (1991), at a forensic inpatient service, developed a programme using a psychoeducational, task-oriented and interactional problem-solving approach to help offenders become more socialized to others and reinforce their commitment to work and leisure pursuits.

Psychologists play an active role in providing psychotherapy in prisons. The aim of individual or group psychotherapy is to facilitate changes in attitude and behaviours of the participant offender (Mathias and Sindberg, 1985; Mathias *et al.*, 1989). Other well-established roles of the psychologist include psychological assessment to provide information about the offender's personality and behavioural characteristics (Grisso, 1986), research (Kohutek, 1983) and in counselling (Deming and Gulliver, 1981–82).

Therapeutic reactors focus on the need for recreational programming within the forensic system. This includes the provision of recreational activities and leisure counselling (Jewell, 1977; Munson, 1991).

There is a need for health professionals working in forensic psychiatry to further define their roles and to publish what they are contributing to this area of practice.

ASPECTS OF SERVICE DELIVERY

There are a number of features about working in a secure environment which create a different working environment from a general psychiatric hospital. Broadly, these centre around security limitations, the nature of the client group and staff attitude.

Security limitations

Goyert (1991) discusses how institutional protocol complicates the delivery of treatment services: prisoners have limitations on movement and have to be escorted to treatment. This treatment could be disrupted if an incident occurred which required the facility to be locked down. Additional problems were long waiting lists for treatment, low referrals for treatment, lack of confidentiality and privacy, poor continuity of treatment, treatment rooms being multipurpose and used by a variety of health care professionals, manipulative patients, and the attitude of management (Schneider, 1979).

There are a number of difficulties associated with providing a treatment service such as psychotherapy in a prison setting. Often, psychotherapy is not voluntary, and other difficulties may include lack of adequate space and furnishings, lack of confidentiality, and lack of trust and unwillingness of the offender-patients to reveal much about themselves (Mathias and Sindberg, 1985; Schlesinger, 1979; Smith and Berlin, 1980).

In secure environments, health care and security are often viewed as opposing forces (Reeder and Meldman, 1991). In secure settings there is a need for the health professional to be security-conscious. Programmes need to be designed for individuals without endangering the physical well-being of the residents and staff. An additional problem is that security personnel can destroy a programme if they so desire: there is a high level of security personnel as compared with health professionals and they often devalue the health care service that is being provided (Jewell, 1977).

Client group

Forensic clients who have been committed involuntarily to a forensic facility are subject to a different release criteria from other client groups. This can result in extended hospital stays and frustration and disappointment if there are delays in release (Miller *et al.*, 1989). The offender-patient is then quite likely to see the therapist as being impotent in giving assistance which may lead to resentment against the therapist, and a severed therapeutic alliance. Treatment becomes difficult in that situation and staff may face frustration and conflict since, in general, treatment staff are oriented towards active treatment (Miller *et al.*, 1989).

An offender-patient population may have a predominance of patients suffering from personality disorder or developmental delay which will have an impact on service delivery. This population may also display chronicity, low self-esteem, and have severe difficulties in relating to others (Gunn and Taylor, 1983).

In the special hospitals in England and Wales there is a high percentage of psychopathic offender-clients who have committed serious crimes of violence. These are a difficult client group to treat. Questions tend to be raised: how does one know when the condition is alleviated? does treatment work? should this group of offender-patients even be in the special hospitals rather than in prison? (Chiswick, 1987). An additional feature of special hospital clients is the high rate of deliberate self-harming (Burrow, 1992).

Staff attitude

It is possible in the secure environment for staff to fall under the influence of powerful sociopathic clients which in turn may lead to breaches in security.

The behaviour of violent and acting-out clients can lead to the staff responding with fright or fear. There are traditional dynamics that result from serious aggression where the aggressor is overcome by force. This display of staff power is enjoyed by some clients because it keeps intact their reputations as powerful threats (Maier, 1986).

Attitudes towards working with confined clients tend to be polarized, i.e. overly authoritarian or excessively benevolent (Maier, 1986). This tends to cause conflict in staff as to how to handle the clients.

Recently there has been an increase of violent and sexual threats to nurses. Fear and concern for personal well-being results in stress and frustration for the staff as this conflicts with their duty of care (Mason, 1991). It has been found that both nursing staff and clients are affected by the potential for violence in secure settings (Caplan, 1993).

Empathy and concern for the welfare of the individual is required; however, countertransference may be generated more easily in a forensic setting than in other settings. The setting requires a high degree of professionalism, paying attention to the burn-out syndrome in order to maintain empathy, resisting being punitive, adjusting to fear and achieving understanding (Ciccone and Clements, 1984).

Role conflict within the forensic setting is common. Conflict is the tension that is generated whenever opposing forces disagree over substantial issues, for example, treatment versus security (Niskala, 1987). Intrapersonal conflict exists when there is incompatibility between a person's beliefs, values, and role expectations. Additional forms of conflict include errors in understanding, dispute over scarce resources such as staff positions, office space, and supplies, role disputes regarding professional territory, misunderstanding of information, tension, and transference. The cost of this type of conflict is high in terms of behavioural, emotional and physical stress responses (Gibson, 1986).

In order to provide an effective forensic psychiatric service staff need to be assisted in having more theoretical knowledge, in-service training, group discussion, clinical supervision, staff selection, staffing procedures, and an awareness of burn-out.

FUTURE DIRECTIONS

Legal reform in the mental health legislations field is known as *legalism*. According to Bradford (1990) the trend towards legalism may result in the reversal of the diversion process which assumes that the individual is better off in the mental health system than in the criminal justice system. This trend may not prove to be in the individual's best interest. Another aspect of the new legalism is the affect that these procedures will have on health care and legal costs.

If, however, court diversion schemes become more frequently utilized in the future, health professionals will increasingly need to look at consultation with other community services (Parry, 1991).

Clients returning to the community from secure settings require a higher degree of support and follow-up than many other client groups (Chaloner and Kinsella, 1992; Parry, 1991). Health professionals are faced with the challenge of developing after-care services to help maintain these clients in the community.

There has been a dramatic growth in scientific knowledge which is providing new information about the biological side of mental illness. There is a challenge for health professionals to increase their understanding of the biological side of mental illness. There is a need for health professionals to increase their understanding of the biological sciences and yet retain their skills in psychosocial treatment (Lowery, 1992). A biopsychological focus may become the focus of psychiatry.

Health professionals will need to look at their practice, their education, and their research in order to prepare for any changes in the care of the mentally abnormal offender. Adequate research uses a scientific method. Ethics in psychiatric research will continue to be an issue (Eichelman *et al.*, 1984). Forensic psychiatry is an area where there is a very definite need for further research (Gunn, 1986).

Models of care adopted from areas outside of forensic psychiatry do not always work in the secure setting owing to its complex nature and environmental features. According to Mason and Chandley (1990), there needs to be a theoretical framework suitable to narrowing the theory/practice gap in the forensic setting.

Another direction that is beginning to emerge is that of education for health professionals in forensic psychiatry. It is hoped that more educational programmes both at the undergraduate and graduate level will be developed.

SUMMARY

Forensic psychiatry represents a unique challenge for health professionals. Changes have taken place in the care and management of the mentally abnormal offender and more changes will take place. It becomes increasingly important for health professionals to develop skills and expertise in working with this group of clients.

REFERENCES

Arboleda-Florez, J. (1981) Forensic psychiatry services in Canada – strengths and weaknesses. *International Journal of Law and Psychiatry*, **4**, 391–9.

Birk, S. (1992) Emerging specialties expand opportunities. *The American Nurse*, **24**, 7,9,24.

Bluglass, R. (1990) The mental health act 1983, in *Principles and Practice of Forensic Psychiatry*, (eds R. Bluglass and P. Bowden), Churchill Livingstone, London, pp. 1173–87.

Bluglass, R. (1981) Advances in forensic psychiatry in England and Wales. *International Journal of Law and Psychiatry*, **4**, 199–212.

Bradford, J. (1990) Mental health legislation in Canada, in *Principles and Practice of Forensic Psychiatry*, (eds R. Bluglass and P. Bowden), Churchill Livingstone, London, pp. 1211–6.

Burrow, S. (1991) Special hospitals – Therapy versus custody. *Nursing Times*, **87**, 64–6.

Burrow, S. (1992) The deliberate self-harming behaviour of patients within a British special hospital. *Journal of Advanced Nursing*, **17**, 138–48.

Caplan, C. (1993) Nursing staff and patient perceptions of the ward atmosphere in a maximum security setting. *Archives of Psychiatric Nursing*, **7**, 23–9.

Chaloner, C. and Kinsella, C. (1992) Care with conviction. *Nursing Times*, **88**, 50–2.

Chaplow, D. (1992) Overview of Auckland regional forensic services: Systems, people and facilities. Conference proceedings, *Progress in Forensic Psychiatry*, Auckland.

Chiswick, D. (1987) Managing psychopathic offenders: A problem that will not go away. *British Medical Journal*, **295**, 159–60.

Ciccone, J. and Clements, C. (1984) Forensic psychiatry and applied clinical ethics: Theory and practice. *American Journal of Psychiatry*, 395–9.

Cook, I. (1991) Springing the trap. *Nursing Times*, **87**, 16–7.

Corden, J. and Clifton, M. (1985) Helping socially isolated prisoners. *British Journal of Social Work*, **15**, 331–50.

Deming, A. and Gulliver, K. (1981–82) Career planning in prison: Ex-inmates help inmates. *Vocational Guidance Quarterly,* **30,** 78–83.

Eichelman, B., Wikler, D. and Hartwig, A. (1984) Ethics and psychiatric research: Problems and justification. *American Journal of Psychiatry,* **141,** 400–5.

Gibson, D. (1985–86). Theory and strategies for resolving conflict. *Occupational Therapy in Mental Health,* **5,** 47–62.

Goyert, P. (1991) Physiotherapy behind bars: A challenge in rehabilitation. *Physiotherapy Canada,* **42,** 40–3.

Grisso, T. (1986) Psychological assessment in legal contexts, in *Forensic Psychiatry and Psychology: Perspectives and Standards for Interdisciplinary Practice,* (eds W. Curran, A. McGarry and S. Shah), F.A. Davis Company, Philadelphia, pp. 103–28.

Gunn, J. (1986) Education and forensic psychiatry, *Canadian Journal of Psychiatry,* **31,** 273–81.

Gunn, J. and Taylor, P. (1983) Rehabilitation of the mentally abnormal offender, in *Theory and Practice of Psychiatric Rehabilitation,* (eds. F. Watts and D. Bennett), John Wiley and Sons, Chichester, pp. 115–28.

Hinton, N. (1976) Social work in prisons. *Health and Social Service Journal,* **86,** 1122–3.

Jewell, D. (1977) Maximum security: Some obstacles of meaningful recreational programming. *Therapeutic Recreation Journal,* **11,** 184–8.

Jones, M. (1953) *The Therapeutic Community,* Basic Books, New York.

Jones, E. and McColl, M. (1991) Development and evaluation of an interactional life skills group for offenders. *The Occupational Therapy Journal of Research,* **11,** 80–92.

Kohutek, K. (1983) Bibliotherapy within a correctional setting. *Journal of Clinical Psychology,* **39,** 920–4.

Lloyd, C. (1984) Trends in forensic psychiatry. Conference proceedings, *Developing Opportunities,* London.

Lowery, B. (1992) Psychiatric nursing in the 1990s and beyond. *Journal of Psychosocial Nursing,* **30,** 7–13.

Lynch, V. (1991) Forensic nursing in the emergency department: A new role for the 1990s. *Critical Care Nursing Quarterly,* **14,** 69–86.

Maier, G. (1986) Relationship security: The dynamics of keepers and kept. *Journal of Forensic Sciences,* **31,** 603–8.

Mason, P. (1991) Violent trends. *Nursing Times,* **87,** 16–7.

Mason, T. and Chandley, M. (1990) Nursing models in a special hospital: A critical analysis of efficacity. *Journal of Advanced Nursing,* **15,** 667–73.

Mathias, R., Mathews, J. and Sindberg, R. (1989) Programs for prisons: Nihilism or pragmatic planning. *International Journal of Offender Therapy and Comparative Criminology,* **33,** 141–8.

Mathias, R. and Sindberg, R. (1985) Psychotherapy in correctional settings. *International Journal of Offender Therapy and Comparative Criminology,* **29,** 265–75.

McCann, G. (1991) Special hospitals – Involving the family. *Nursing Times,* **87,** 67–8.

Miller, R., Maier, G., Van Rybroek, G. and Weidemann, J. (1989) Treating Patients 'doing time': A forensic perspective. *Hospital and Community Psychiatry*, **40**, 960–2.

Munson, W. (1991) Juvenile delinquency as a societal problem and social disability: The therapeutic recreator's role as ecological change agent. *Therapeutic Recreation Journal*, **25**, 19–30.

Niskala, H. (1986) Competencies and skills required by nurses working in forensic areas. *Western Journal of Nursing Research*, **8**, 400–13.

Niskala, H. (1987) Conflicting convictions: Nurses in forensic settings. *Canadian Journal of Psychiatric Nursing*, **28**, 10–4.

O'Brien, K. and Branson, C. (1990) Australasia: Law and services, in *Principles and Practice of Forensic Psychiatry*, (eds R. Bluglass and P. Bowden), Churchill Livingstone, London, pp. 1225–34.

Parry, J. (1991) Community care for mentally ill offenders. *Nursing Standard*, **5**, 29–33.

Platt, N., Martell, D. and Clements, P. (1977) Level 1 field placement at a federal correctional institution. *American Journal of Occupational Therapy*, **31**, 385–7.

Reeder, D. and Meldman, L. (1991) Conceptualizing psychosocial nursing in the jail setting. *Journal of Psychosocial Nursing*, **29**, 40–4.

Roffe, K. (1992) The national maximum security of New Zealand 'container to service'. Conference proceedings, *Progress in Forensic Psychiatry*, Auckland, pp. 123–8.

Rogers, C. (1951) *Client-centred Therapy*, Constable, London.

Rossenrode, P. and Cottingham, C. (1992) A New Zealand graduate certificate course in forensic psychiatry. Conference proceedings, *Progress in Forensic Psychiatry*, Auckland, pp. 14–6.

Schlesinger, S. (1979) Therapy on a treadmill: The role of the prison psychotherapist. *Professional Psychology*, **10**, 307–17.

Schneider, M. (1979) Problems in short term correctional settings. *International Journal of Offender Therapy and Comparative Criminology*, **23**, 164–71.

Smith, B. and Berlin, L. (1980) The place of psychotherapy in probation and parole: The patient as offender, in *Forensic Psychology and Psychiatry*, (eds F. Wright, C. Bahn and R. Rieber), New York Academy of Sciences, New York, pp. 157–66.

Snowden, P. (1985) A survey of the regional secure unit programme. *British Journal of Psychiatry*, **147**, 499–507.

Stein, L. and Diamond, R. (1985) The chronically mentally ill and the criminal justice system: When to call the police. *Hospital and Community Psychiatry*, **36**, 271–4.

Taylor, P. (1988) Forensic psychiatry. *British Journal of Psychiatry*, **153**, 271–8.

2

Types of settings

Legal aspects are of importance in understanding the ramifications for treatment. However, the nature and structure of the setting determines how services are offered. Settings vary greatly, not only in different countries but also within a country. This has to do for the main part with historical development, trends in legislation and the perceived requirements for treating the mentally abnormal offender. Settings may be as diverse as prisons, maximum security hospitals such as the special hospitals, secure units in local psychiatric hospitals, general hospital forensic units, special treatment units and community forensic services.

This chapter aims to look at a number of different forensic settings and how the setting itself has an impact on what may happen for the institutionalized individual. Psychological aspects of institutionalization, in addition to the types of services available and the attitude of staff towards them, are all powerful influences on individuals. This chapter explores:

- total institutions
- maximum security settings: prisons
- maximum security settings: special hospitals
- local mental hospitals: secure units
- general hospitals: forensic units
- special treatment units
- community forensic services and
- staff issues.

Health professionals working in forensic psychiatry require a broad base of knowledge to understand the complexities of the setting, legal issues, the client group, and the impact of the environment. This is essential since a combination of biology, pathology, philosophy, and sociology constitute forensic psychiatry (Gunn, 1986).

Once mentally abnormal offenders are institutionalized, their primary social group becomes the institution. Extended institutionalization alters community ties and social relationships. The cultural environment has a pervasive impact on the individual (Barris *et al.*, 1985).

For an overall perspective on the effects of total institutions such as forensic settings, Rossenrode and Cottingham (1992) suggest reading Goffman's *Asylums* (1961), with its still valid description of the effects of that particular cultural milieu. A brief overview of total institutions is outlined below.

TOTAL INSTITUTIONS

According to Goffman (1961), the basic social arrangement in contemporary society is that an individual tends to sleep, play, and work in different settings with different participants, usually of their own choice.

A central feature of total institutions is the breakdown of the barriers that ordinarily separate these activities so that all three activities take place in the same setting with the same people; there is an absence of free choice.

Goffman (1961) examines four characteristics that are necessary if an institution is to be classified as a total institution. These include:

- all aspects of the individual's life are conducted in the same place and under the same authority;
- each of the individual's daily activities is carried out in the immediate company of a large number of others, all of whom are treated alike and are required to do the same things;
- all of the day's activities are tightly scheduled, with each leading at a pre-arranged time to the next, and with the sequence of events being imposed by authority from above; and

- all activities are rationally planned and carried out for the sake of the institution.

Mental hospitals, prisons, and forensic psychiatric facilities may be viewed as total institutions in the light of the characteristics Goffman outlined. They can be categorized as existing in order to protect society against those who are potentially dangerous, who may be a threat to the community, or who may be incapable of taking care of themselves.

Goffman (1961) argues that common to total institutions is the fact that individuals in such institutions undergo a process of 'self-mortification'. This process which involves interacting with others in the institutional setting, strips the individual of his identity. It is also implied that this mortification of the self occurs regardless of how therapeutic or non-therapeutic the environment of the total institution.

Goffman (1961) identifies the features of an institutional environment that he suggests contribute to the mortification process:

- Admission procedures typically bring about a series of losses. The individual is often stripped of personal possessions, and may be issued institutional clothing. Such procedures are depersonalizing in that they serve to detach the individual from the social system at large. Depersonalization also occurs through symbolic means for example, being addressed as 'you'.
- The total institution places barriers between the individual and the outside world that result in a loss of roles that are an important part of the individual's personal identity. Both the quantity and quality of interactions with family and significant others is most obviously affected. A number of restrictions may apply, for example, reduced visiting hours, retrictions on minors visiting, telephone access is often limited, letters may be read. Most significantly, all institutional persons face the loss of a way of living.
- Because total institutions deal with almost all aspects of the individual's life, there is a need to obtain co-operation. The individual may be required to show deference to staff or face the consequences for failing to do so; this results in a loss of self-esteem for the individual.

- Verbal or physical humiliation may occur. Individuals may have to beg or humbly ask for things, for example, permission to use the phone. Staff or fellow residents may abuse the person and there may be a loss of a sense of personal safety.
- In the community, individuals can hold on to feelings about self, actions, thoughts, and possessions from others if they so choose. In the total institution, these areas of self are violated. Facts about the person are collected upon admission and continually recorded and made available to staff. Individuals have no choice in their surroundings, have forced social relationships and experience a loss of privacy.

Being aware of the mortification process is an important consideration for health professionals working in these types of settings. It increases understanding of what occurs for mentally abnormal offenders and their loss of personal identity, role, and social relationships that they'd previously enjoyed.

MAXIMUM SECURITY SETTINGS

Prisons

Maximum security settings in which treatment takes place occurs in both the penal and health service systems. Many prisons have a hospital wing for the care of psychiatric as well as physical disorders. In other prisons a special unit has been incorporated to house mentally abnormal offenders. In some instances, prison management contracts in health care workers to provide treatment for offenders as required, otherwise health professionals are hired to work in the unit.

With increases in the prison population there has been an increasing number of mentally abnormal offenders (Bluglass, 1981; Gunn and Taylor, 1983). A number of explanations have been offered for this trend.

In the USA, according to Reeder and Meldman (1991), the trend towards deinstitutionalization of state mental hospitals, more restrictive commitment standards, and court-ordered minimum standards for medical and mental health services has had an impact on prisons. There is an increase in the rate of mentally ill offenders ending up in prisons rather than in mental hospitals.

According to Stein and Diamond (1985), prisons have been used increasingly to get non-committable persons with chronic mental illness off the streets and into a protective environment. They cite the reason for this has resulted from the failure to develop adequate community-based services for chronic mentally ill persons. Goldmeier *et al.*, (1986) found that it was difficult to encourage community mental health centres to take greater interest in forensic clients owing to lack of resources to deal with potentially dangerous persons.

In a study conducted by Robertson (1988) to examine arrests among the mentally ill he found that the majority were homeless, wandering abroad, and were displaying florid psychotic symptoms. These persons were remanded into custody for offences that in other circumstances would have resulted in bail being granted.

The majority of inmates serving time in prisons are not mentally ill. In fact, only a small percentage of inmates suffer from well-defined severe psychiatric disorder such as the psychoses. This has been suggested to be less than 5% of the total prison population (Roth, 1986). Mentally ill offenders are an underserved population and are at risk for further deterioration of their mental status. Another 15% of the total prison population may require therapeutic intervention at some time. Emotional stress is a key feature of this group of offenders. Acute anxiety and acute depression may be present which may result in the offender attempting suicide, self-mutilation, displaced violence, panic, or social withdrawal (Roth, 1986).

Offenders seen in prisons vary greatly. They may be dangerous criminals, first-time or habitual offenders, offenders who experience stress reaction to being incarcerated, offenders with a previous psychiatric history and sentenced offenders who become mentally ill. Once people become inmates of a prison they experience a loss of identity and a loss of control which creates a continual state of crisis (Adams, 1985).

It can seldom be said that the time an inmate spends being incarcerated is constructive. The prison subculture is an undeniably powerful force. Inmates are very susceptible to a variety of pressures being placed on them by their fellow inmates (Roth, 1986). Violence is common and usually associated with such things as sexual exploitation, racial tensions, religious and cultural differences, fighting over cigarettes, drugs or contraband, enforcement of debts, pay-offs to informers, and being members of rival prison cliques. Additionally, those inmates who have been convicted of violent crimes are, in particular, very sensitive to others invading their personal space (Roth, 1986).

Short-term facilities have many of the problems associated with the larger more isolated prisons. They have a number of additional problems which include a rapid turnover of the inmate population; destruction of institutional property; a large variety of offence categories; lack of jobs to occupy inmates; acute emotional stress; lack of opportunity for staff to become thoroughly familiar with inmates and the problems they may be experiencing, and the frequency of recidivism that tends to discourage staff (Petrich, 1976).

Having been stripped of the identity of self in the outside world, rights and social roles, and left in a state of helplessness, many inmates reach a state of desocialization and must try and re-evaluate themselves in order to define their new roles. They develop a redefinition of their self-concept based upon the prison social system (Rosenfield and Linn, 1976).

Overcrowding exacerbates the stresses of institutional life and compounds the inherent problems of prisons (Bluglass, 1981). These problems are most likely to relate to poor living conditions, sharing cells, lack of privacy and of meaningful activities, violence between inmates, sexual abuse, and exploitation (Flynn, 1976; Roth, 1986). Progressive overcrowding leads to violence between inmates. The prison setting is a stressful environment, even for those who have previously served time (Arboleda-Florez, 1981; Marcus and Alcabes, 1993).

Any one of a number of factors can contribute towards breakdowns for inmates . These include hearing bad news from home, loss of family support, visits being missed, being placed in segregation following an infraction of rules and regulations, victimization or fighting with other inmates and thwarted probation/parole hopes. Confinement, in particular, segregation and lack of stimulation are well-known stressors that can lead to a psychotic episode (Arboleda-Florez, 1981). Depending on the coping abilities of the inmates, the likelihood of breakdowns will occur with varying frequency and intensity. Psychosocial consequences include anger, anxiety, depression, despair and learned helplessness (Petrich, 1976).

Health care professionals in prisons must be alert to the high potential for suicidal behaviour among inmates (Marcus and Alcabes, 1993). Suicide is another aspect of how an inmate chooses to deal with the situation. Suicide is the leading cause of death in most penal settings. It is estimated that the incidence of suicide in penal settings is three times greater than the national average (Hatty, 1988). The risk of successfully committing suicide is far greater at the time of initial incarceration or pre-trial than later on during a prison sentence. The inmates who attempt or successfully commit suicide are quite often drug or alcohol users. Hanging is the most frequent method used, with the high-risk times being at night or early morning when there are less staff available for observation (Backett, 1987; Topp, 1979).

According to Roth (1986), the following profiles are at risk for suicide: 1) a young, impulsive inmate charged with a violent crime who cannot deal with confinement; 2) a somewhat older inmate who has a past psychiatric history and is clinically depressed; 3) a respectable member of the community who is charged with a first offence and cannot face the shame of going to prison; and 4) a chronic offender who cannot face doing any more time.

To be effective and useful in delivery of health care within prison-based services, it is important to be knowledgeable about the special aspects of being involved in health care in a prison. In some ways the concept of therapy and that of guarding the prisoner are diametrically opposed. There are divergent aims between and among prison administration, prison staff, inmates, and health care staff (Reeder and Meldman, 1991). This naturally may lead to conflict as the underlying assumptions of the parties involved in the care and custody of the inmates differ. The prison is faced with the task of producing positive change in the context of a partially negative environment (Rosenfield and Linn, 1976).

Farmer (1977) found significant role problems for custodial staff who work in treatment institutions. It was found that in principle they agreed with the idea of treatment or rehabilitation but were nevertheless cynical about the outcome. The prison staff are caught in the middle between a sense of security and custody and an idea of treatment.

The question of rehabilitation of inmates has been debated over the years (Wright, 1980). Bluglass (1981) suggests that a more restrictive punitive approach seems to be in favour. Some people argue that it is not possible to put into operation a rehabilitation programme within the institutional setting and that the reason people go to prison is for punishment and for the protection of people and property in the community, not for rehabilitation (Wright, 1980). Others believe that inmates should have the right for rehabilitation and treatment if required (Jones and McColl, 1991). The actual aims of imprisonment may interfere with the provision of health care, for instance, health care may be witheld as a form of punishment or may not be seen as being important (Goyert, 1991; Jewell, 1977).

The health care worker should provide a service that is inmate oriented, and that provides the most appropriate therapeutic intervention for the particular or specific needs of the inmate, rather than taking undue notice of the nature of the crime, parole concerns or whether or not an inmate recidivates (Roth, 1986; Taylor, 1985). The challenge lies in the ability to advocate for adequate accessibility and availability of health care according to health needs of the individual without becoming involved in a power struggle or being manipulated (Reeder and Meldman, 1991).

A close working relationship between the health care staff and the non-medical prison staff is critical in successfully implementing an early diagnostic and treatment service. Otherwise offenders in need of psychiatric treatment may be overlooked, identified as troublemakers or simply dismissed as manipulative individuals who are unworthy of attention (James *et al.*, 1980; Petrich, 1976).

A strong solid foundation in crisis intervention theory and techniques is useful in the prison setting. Short-term supportive therapy along with helping the inmates deal with the uncertainty and loss of control is necessary (Reeder and Meldman, 1991). Staff require a creative approach using a humanist, non-judgemental philosophy. Marcus and Alcabes (1993) suggest that systems for prompt identification, evaluation and treatment of offenders who are at risk can be effective in the delivery of care.

Special hospitals

As well as the penal system, mentally abnormal offenders are to be found in health service facilities and in the special hospitals. Maximum security hospitals exist in most countries throughout the world. The reason that mentally abnormal offenders are placed in maximum security hospitals is because of their perceived level of dangerousness. It is the combination of mental disorder and dangerous behaviour which warrants secure surroundings. This group of patients tend to be those who constitute a serious public risk by having killed someone, wounded a person, being sexually assaultive or committed arson (Black, 1984).

The behaviour categories and the mental disorders associated with them will vary from one special hospital to the next. According to Black (1984), apart from psychopathic disorder and mental handicap, most of the patients seen in special hospitals will be classified as some form of schizophrenic or depressive or else neurotic or paranoid personality disorder.

Bullard (1992) found that clients who continue to require treatment in maximum security fall into four main categories: clients with chronic schizophrenia whose illness has not responded to treatment; those suffering from chronic schizophrenia who have not responded to treatment and who remain psychotic and persistently assaultive; young female clients suffering from psychopathic disorder who have a history of sexual and physical abuse, and the sexual psychopath who has a history of serious and often recidivist sexual offending.

Offender-patients are treated according to how they behave and there is not the same degree of loss of personal identity, loss of self-respect, and feelings of powerlessness that tends to take place in the prison setting. People serving their time in prison are there to serve the sentence they received for their criminal acts. During this time their lives are under conditions of total control. Special hospitals differ in the fact that, although clients are likewise under conditions of control, they are there in order to undergo treatment, not to serve sentences of imprisonment (Burrow, 1991).

The emphasis on treatment in a special hospital focuses on educational, occupational and recreational programmes. The milieu thus provided creates a constant stimulus in addition to a constant support and reference point for patients who on the whole have been deprived of the presence of a supportive family and social network (Black, 1984).

Many kinds of clients, on reaching the rehabilitative stage of their treatment, need to experience a wider range of more normal, less restricted environments. In the special hospitals, it is difficult to achieve the graded transition to an environment approximating the normal world outside the hospital without jeopardizing the control which is an essential part of the special hospitals' purpose. Rehabilitation is often difficult to organize owing to the special hospitals' remote locations and the reluctance of psychiatric facilities to take special hospital clients (Gunn and Taylor, 1983). It has been found that many of the clients transferred from special hospitals to regional secure units fail and are returned to special hospitals (Burrow, 1991).

The move out of the special hospital is not one that takes place very quickly. Discharge or transfer out of a special hospital, even if only for a period of trial leave inevitably takes time. Various possibilities have to be explored and arranged, necessary precautions specified and authorization obtained (Black, 1984).

Lengthy delays can set back, and in fact can even undo the progress made in treatment up to that point. This then affects the success of the next phase of treatment. Additionally, the therapist must at some level be seen by the client as being involved in preventing him or her from discharge from the special hospital to next stage of treatment or rehabilitation. This inevitably colours the therapeutic relationship as the client may be reluctant to trust the therapist and disclose material which the client fears may hinder discharge (Miller *et al.*, 1989).

The maintenance of security in the special hospitals rests solely with the staff – both nursing and other health professionals – who provide treatment. The underlying reason for this is that security is best maintained when staff are in regular contact with their clients and come to know them sufficiently well that they are able to monitor and anticipate any potential security risks that a clients' changing condition may present (Black, 1984). Staff numbers have increased and there is a high client:staff ratio (Dyer 1991).

A number of questions have been raised concerning the large maximum security hospitals, the methods of treatment, the handling of violent and dangerous behaviour, the use of seclusion, and the problems of rehabilitation (Bluglass, 1981; Burrow, 1991). It has been suggested that 50% of the clients are inappropriately placed in maximum security hospitals as they do not need that level of security (Bullard, 1992; Dell *et al.*, 1987). Dyer (1991) has gone as far as to state that the special hospitals should be phased out altogether.

LOCAL MENTAL HOSPITALS

Secure units

A trend that is particularly evident in countries such as Britain, the United States, Canada, New Zealand, and Australia are the gradually developing forensic units which are not envisaged to meet the criterion of maximum security; varying levels of security being minimum or medium will be put in place.

Local mental hospitals do not necessarily take offender patients. Some do and others do not. The decision rests on hospital policy, the catchment area, and whether or not the hospital has secure facilities. Many psychiatric hospitals nowadays are without a locked ward. Hospitals have also become increasingly reluctant to accept violent acting-out clients. This then has an impact on the movement of special hospital clients. There is some difficulty in persuading psychiatric hospitals to take clients no longer in need of being in a special hospital (Gunn and Taylor, 1983).

Mental hospital psychiatric practice has changed with its open wards and emphasis upon community care for the mentally ill and the development of similar psychiatric units in general hospitals has resulted in a shift in the character of the client population and staff attitudes towards it. With this move towards developing acute psychiatric units in general hospitals, there is often a reluctance to accept potentially violent and aggressive clients (Gunn and Taylor, 1983; Snowden, 1985). Phillips (1983) states that in some psychiatric facilities care for the mentally abnormal offender arouses confusion, fear and consternation.

A number of secure units have already been established to cater for mentally abnormal offenders. Secure units have a number of features in common. They have a high staff:client ratio. Having a greater ratio of staff to clients provides a greater level of security for clients with behaviour disturbances. The secure units provide a range of facilities and services. Programmes are a combination of therapeutic, educational, vocational and recreational. Provision is also made for outpatient and community care so that there is continuity in the service provided. The facilities are purpose-built and provide a secure setting, not to the same degree as the special hospitals, but rather providing varying degrees of security and intensive care according to the many different categories of clients (Snowden, 1985).

The secure units are integrated into the general psychiatric services and are associated with forensic psychiatry centres in the community. It is important that close links be developed with the prison service, the probation service and social service, and to establish a close working relationship with the special hospitals. This would then enable clients to move more easily between one level of security and another as their behaviour, mental state and level of dangerousness dictates (Bluglass, 1981; Dyer, 1991). The whole concept of secure units is more positive, dynamic and therapeutic, and more in keeping with the changing concepts of psychiatric care.

GENERAL HOSPITALS

Forensic units

Arboleda-Florez and Holley (1987) describe a somewhat different approach to the establishment of a secure unit. This particular programme is unique in that it is located within a general hospital psychiatric department rather than in a prison setting or adjacent to a large psychiatric hospital. It is an interesting concept in that in establishing this type of service, the most recent trends in both corrections and community psychiatry have been incorporated.

The outpatient programme includes hospital-based service for traditional outpatients as well as an institutional service for incarcerated offenders. The out-patient staff travel to a variety of institutions and community settings throughout southern Alberta. The aim was to develop a fully integrated service delivery system where a patient would be followed through the various stages of the judicial process, that is, from pre-trial to incarceration to community release (Arboleda-Florez and Holley, 1987).

The in-patient programme is located in a locked security facility which operates to receive pre-trial, pre-sentence, treatment and parole case. The major portion of the work done in the unit relates to pre-trial assessments, particularly to determine fitness to stand trial. It is short-term and there is a high client turnover (Arboleda-Florez and Holley, 1987).

Additionally, an emergency service for acutely ill offenders from the various correctional and penal services is carried out and for some individuals for whom preventative measures might be more appropriate than incarceration they are placed in the forensic treatment programmes. All clients that are seen must have some legal or correctional hold on them (Arboleda-Florez and Holley, 1987).

Special units

Sex offenders (and the nature of the crimes they commit) comprise one group of offenders that has a clear association with a high incidence of psychological deviation. Attempts to develop treatment programmes are particularly appropriate so that, on the offender's return to society, they will not present a major threat to the community (Arboleda-Florez, 1981). A number of different treatment methods have been used, for example individual psychotherapy, group psychotherapy within a therapeutic community setting, behaviour modification techniques for modifying erotic responses and reinforcing social behaviour, and sexual suppressant drugs in conjunction with combined approaches with varying degrees of success (Bluglass, 1981).

Persons convicted of violent offences are a high recidivist group. The cost of violence to the community is high both socially and in criminal justice resources (Dixon and Polaschek, 1992). For this reason some programmes have been established, using therapeutic community principles, to help violent offenders to better control their anger, to learn and apply alternatives to violence and to develop skills that promote acceptable survival in the community (Dixon and Polaschek, 1992).

COMMUNITY FORENSIC SERVICES

Some countries have been active in developing community forensic services. These services are usually a combination of assessment and treatment. For offender-patients who have committed non-violent offences, community forensic services are a valuable option. This means that the person does not have to be institutionalized for treatment but is still provided with the required treatment while living in the community (Gunn and Taylor, 1983).

A well-developed relationship between the probation services and the forensic psychiatric services ensures an integrated approach to care. In treatment programmes, joint strategies can be adopted with the probation services and other services to help offenders who often have serious personal problems or illness (Bluglass, 1981; Bradford, 1990). This is particularly important since many mentally abnormal offenders experience difficulties in a number of areas upon their return to the community (Chaloner and Kinsella, 1992). Clients need to be assisted to maintain their well-being and reduce the risk of their re-offending as a result of a deterioration in their mental state (Parry, 1991).

STAFF ISSUES

Health professionals working in forensic settings have to be actively aware that their parameters are different from those of other psychiatric hospital settings. Extended hospital stays of forensic clients and situations such as the patient being clinically but not legally ready for discharge can lead to severed therapeutic alliances, role confusion, general frustration and conflict and staff-client power struggles (Miller *et al.*, 1989).

Roth (1986) states that there are many strains placed on the role of the health professional in a prison setting. This ranges from doing constant crisis intervention to the attitudes of the inmates and the prison officers. Prison officers sometimes ridicule health care as they view it as ineffective (Roth, 1986). The inmates consider the health professional as one more authority figure they have to deal with. The forensic health professional may appear impotent to a client who is only motivated to work if release is the reward (Miller *et al.*, 1989). Often health professionals are viewed by their clients as being relatively uninfluential in terms of release, transfer and so on and may not co-operate with treatment (Rossenrode and Cottingham, 1992).

There is conflict in the approach to dealing with the mentally abnormal offender (Phillips, 1983). Clients in the forensic system are there involuntarily and there is conflict over opposing interests, particularly related to receiving therapy involuntarily (Christie, 1983). Clients are often unhappy about the situation and reluctant to participate in the treatment programmes (Rossenrode and Cottingham, 1992).

Health professionals need to recognize and acknowledge that there is a basic conflict between the goals of forensic health care and that of security (Niskala, 1986). This often causes confusion and stress for the staff as they try to reconcile these two opposing forces. Health professionals must maintain a therapeutic environment while observing security measures (Caplan, 1993).

Other areas that cause stress and frustration for health professionals in the forensic setting include interruption to programmes (Jewell, 1977; Dyer, 1991), difficulties meeting rehabilitative requirements (Hepworth, 1985) and professional isolation (Roth, 1986).

There is often conflict among health professionals about their role and taking on tasks that other people do not see as their role (Niskala, 1987), or by filling in the gap in the client's programme at the expense of their primary responsibilities (Reed, 1984). As members of a multidisciplinary team, health professionals have clinical skills in common with a number of members of the team. If the team is not well-managed, health professionals may become frustrated and discouraged by role confusion, rivalries and conflicts (Reed, 1984).

SUMMARY

This chapter has looked at a range of different settings where health professionals may be involved in the assessment and treatment of forensic psychiatric clients. The impact of the environment on the individual was examined and the implications this then has for the treatment staff.

REFERENCES

Adams, K. (1985) Addressing inmate mental health problems: A new direction for prison therapeutic services. *Federal Probation*, **49**, 27–33.
Arboleda-Florez, J. (1981) Forensic psychiatry services in Canada: Strengths and weaknesses. *International Journal of Law and Psychiatry*, **4**, 391–9.
Arboleda-Florez, J. and Holley, H. (1987) General hospital forensic units: A new approach to forensic psychiatry. *International Journal of Offender Therapy and Comparative Criminology*, **31**, 11–9.
Backett, S. (1987) Suicide in Scottish prisons. *British Journal of Psychiatry*, **151**, 218–21.
Barris, R., Kielhofner, G., Neville, A. *et al.* (1985) Psychosocial dysfunction, in *A Model of Human Occupation: Theory and Application*, (ed G. Kielhofner), Williams and Wilkins, Baltimore, pp. 248–305.
Black, T. (1984) Treatment in maximum security settings, in *Mentally Abnormal Offenders*, (eds M. Craft and A. Craft), Ballière Tindall, London, pp. 350–83.
Bluglass, R. (1981) Advances in forensic psychiatry in England and Wales. *International Journal of Law and Psychiatry*, **4**, 199–212.
Bradford, J. (1990) Mental health legislation in Canada, in *Principles and Practice of Forensic Psychiatry*, (eds R. Bluglass and P. Bowden), Churchill Livingstone, London, pp. 1211–6.
Bullard, H. (1992) How special are special hospitals? Conference proceedings, *Progress in Forensic Psychiatry*, Auckland, pp. 106–11.
Burrow, S. (1991) Special hospitals: Therapy versus custody. *Nursing Times*, **87**, 64–6.
Caplan, C. (1993) Nursing staff and patient perceptions of the ward atmosphere in a maximum security forensic hospital. *Archives of Psychiatric Nursing*, **7**, 23–9.
Chaloner, C. and Kinsella, C. (1992) Care with conviction. *Nursing Times*, **88**, 50–2.
Christie, N. (1983) Criminological diagnosis: Forensic psychiatry, in *Criminological Diagnosis: An International Perspective, vol 1*, eds (F. Ferracuti and M. Wolfgang), Heath and Company, Massachusetts, pp. 179–85.
Dell, S., Robertson, G. and Parker, E. (1987) Detention in Broadmoor: Factors in length of stay. *British Journal of Psychiatry*, **150**, 824–7.
Dixon, B. and Polaschek, D. (1992) Development and evaluation of a treatment programme for violent offenders, in Conference proceedings, *Progress in Forensic Psychiatry*, Auckland, pp. 94–100.

Dyer, L. (1991) Special Hospitals. *Nursing Times*, **87**, 69.

Farmer, R. (1977) Cynicism: A factor in correctional work. *Journal of Criminal Justice*, **5**, 237–46.

Flynn, E. (1976) The ecology of prison violence, in *Prison Violence*, (eds A. Cohen, G. Cole, and R. Bailey), D.C. Heath and Company, Lexington, Massachusetts, pp. 115–33.

Goffman, E. (1961) *Asylums*, Doubleday & Co., Inc., New York.

Goldmeir, J., Wise, B. and Wright, C. (1986) Forensic social work in a mental health setting. *Health and Social Work*, **11**, 245–53.

Goyert, P. (1991) Physiotherapy behind bars: A challenge in rehabilitation. *Physiotherapy Canada*, **43**, 40–3.

Gunn, J. (1986) Education and forensic psychiatry. *Canadian Journal of Psychiatry*, **31**, 273–80.

Gunn, J. and Taylor, P. (1983) Rehabilitation of the mentally abnormal offender, in *Theory and practice of Psychiatric Rehabilitation*, (eds F. Watts and D. Bennett), John Wiley and Sons, Chichester, pp. 115–28.

Hatty, S. (1988) Suicide in gaol: The construction and measurement of a phenomenon. *Australian Journal of Social Issues*, **23**, 184–95.

Hepworth, D. (1985) Dangerousness and the mental health review tribunal, in *Aggression and Dangerousness*, (eds D. Farrington and J. Gunn), John Wiley & Sons, Chichester, pp. 155–83.

James, J., Gregory, D., Jones, R. *et al.* (1980) Psychiatric morbidity in prisons. *Hospital and Community Psychiatry*, **31**, 674–7.

Jewell, D. (1977) Maximum security: Some obstacles of meaningful recreational programming. *Therapeutic Recreation Journal*, **11**, 184–8.

Jones, E. and McColl, M. (1991) Development and evaluation of an interactional life skills group for offenders. *Occupational Therapy Journal of Research*, **11**, 80–92.

Marcus, P. and Alcabes, P. (1993) Characteristics of suicides by inmates in an urban jail. *Hospital and Community Psychiatry*, **44**, 256–61.

Miller, R., Maier, G., Van Rybroek, G. *et al.* (1989) Treating patients 'doing time': A forensic perspective. *Hospital and Community Psychiatry*, **40**, 960–2.

Niskala, H. (1986) Competencies and skills required by nurses working in forensic areas. *Western Journal of Nursing Research*, **8**, 400–13.

Niskala, H. (1987) Conflicting convictions. *Canadian Journal of Psychiatric Nursing*, **28**, 10–4.

Parry, J. (1991) Community care for mentally ill offenders. *Nursing Standard*, **5**, 29–33.

Petrich, J. (1976) Psychiatric treatment in Jail: An experiment in health-care delivery. *Hospital and Community Psychiatry*, **27**, 413–5.

Phillips, M. (1983) Forensic psychiatry. *Dimensions in Health Service*, **60**, 41–3.

Reed, S. (1984) Occupational therapists in the interdisciplinary team setting, in *The Changing Roles of Occupational Therapists in the 1980s*, (ed. F. Cromwell), The Haworth Press, New York, pp. 59–66.

Reeder, D. and Meldman, L. (1991) Conceptualizing psychosocial nursing in the jail setting. *Journal of Psychosocial Nursing*, **29**, 40–4.

Robertson, G. (1988) Arrest patterns among mentally disordered offenders. *British Journal of Psychiatry*, **153**, 313, 316.

Rosenfield, J. and Linn, M. (1976) Perceptions of penal environment and attitude change. *Journal of Clinical Psychology*, **32**, 548–53.

Rossenrode, P. and Cottingham, C. (1992) A New Zealand graduate certificate course in forensic psychiatry, in Conference proceedings, *Progress in Forensic Psychiatry*, Auckland, pp. 14–6.

Roth, L. (1986) Correctional psychiatry, in *Forensic Psychiatry and Psychology: Perspectives and Standards for Interdisciplinary Practice*, (eds W. Curran, A. McGarry, and S. Shah), F.A. Davis Company, Philadelphia, pp. 429–68.

Snowden, P. (1985) A survey of the regional secure unit programme. *British Journal of Psychiatry*, **147**, 499–507.

Stein, L. and Diamond, R. (1985) The chronically mentally ill and the criminal justice system: When to call the police. *Hospital and Community Psychiatry*, **36**, 271–4.

Taylor, P. (1985) Motives for offending among violent and psychotic men. *British Journal of Psychiatry*, **147**, 491–8.

Topp, D. (1979) Suicide in prison. *British Journal of Psychiatry*, **134**, 24–7.

Wright, K. (1980) A re-examination of correctional alternatives. *International Journal of Offender Therapy and Comparative Criminology*, **24**, 179–92.

3

The client population

INTRODUCTION

Clients may range from those seen for assessment purposes only to those who require treatment. There are clients requiring only minimum or medium security; other clients may be severely disruptive, display dangerous behaviour, may be mentally ill, mentally handicapped or have a severe personality disorder and may require maximum security (Tse, 1990). In addition, there are specific groups of clients such as psychopaths who pose a controversial treatment issue, and special needs minority groups such as women, the elderly, the mentally handicapped offender and AIDS sufferers who should be considered as they each have their own unique set of problems. Treatment issues surrounding this group of clients are complex and multifaceted; they are complicated by environmental and social factors.

This chapter looks at client features and health needs that the health professional may consider when providing assessment and treatment services in forensic settings. This chapter explores:

- dangerous offenders
- psychopathic offenders
- women offenders
- the elderly offender
- the mentally handicapped offender
- the offender with Acquired Immune Deficiency Syndrome (AIDS)
- offenders requiring after care.

According to Johnson (1986) wellness is perceived as a dynamic way of life in which good health habits are incorporated into an individual's life to improve both health and quality of life. Awareness of the client's total health needs provides direction for health professionals in designing treatment programmes to help their clients achieve a state of wellness and life satisfaction.

DANGEROUS OFFENDERS

Taylor (1985) found that immediate retaliation to perceived provocation was the most common reason for offending for both psychotic and non-psychotic offenders. With the non-psychotic offenders motives included high emotional arousal, for example, panic, self-defence, morbid jealousy and immediate retaliation were more likely to be associated with serious violence. In the psychotic group, delusions were relatively common precipitants for offending. Taylor (1985) suggests that the importance of delusional drive in relation to seriously violent offending may be higher than previously thought. Benezech *et al.* (1980) found that paranoids, paranoid schizophrenics, and undifferentiated schizophrenics were much more often hospitalized for violent crimes than the population with other psychiatric diagnoses. In a study conducted by Zitrin and associates (1976) they found that re-arrest rates were higher for ex-patients than for the general population. Benezech *et al.* (1980) suggest that the best prediction of future arrest was prior arrest.

Mentally ill offenders, mainly schizophrenics, treated in maximum security facilities will receive the standard drug treatment and the extent to which the illness can be controlled has implications for transfer to a less restrictive environment (Dell *et al.*, 1987).

It has been found that factors relating to the seriousness and chronicity of the mentally abnormal offenders' illness was a relevant factor in the length of stay in a maximum security facility (Dell *et al.*, 1987).

An important consideration when looking at psychotic offenders is that many of them at the time of the offence were disorganized, socially isolated and homeless (Robertson, 1988; Taylor, 1985). Robertson (1988) suggests that the social incompetence and debilitated state of this group of offenders makes them vulnerable to detection and detention. Treatment programmes may need to focus on such areas as social skills training, skills training in activities of daily living, money management, supportive psychotherapy, recreational therapy, educational and vocational training and behavioural approaches such as desensitization and behaviour modification.

Violent, mentally abnormal juveniles are a small group of offenders who inflict considerable harm to the community both in terms of violence and fear (Hartstone and Cocozza, 1983). These offenders are likely to have previously been to court, have prior violent offences, usually have had prior residential placements, and are likely to be psychotic (Hartstone and Cocozza, 1983). They have a high recidivism rate; the majority of those released into the community have re-offended within the year. Hartstone and Cocozza (1983) suggest that the first few months after release are critical ones for recidivism.

This group of clients characteristically displays low self-esteem, poor impulse control, disturbed interpersonal relationships, incomplete schooling, lack of a trade and limited or non-existent work experience. Treatment options may include a focus on individual and group psychotherapy, family counselling, educational upgrading, recreational activities, vocational therapy, anger management and personal development.

The proportion of violent offenders amongst those imprisoned has increased. Persons convicted of violent offences are a high recidivist group (Dixon and Polaschek, 1992). Offences may include murder, attempted murder, manslaughter, assault and sexual assault. This group of clients may display deficits in heterosocial skills, poor control over feelings of anger and hostility, low self-esteem, and, depending on the offence, may also display sexually anomalous behaviour. Dixon and Polaschek (1992) suggest that effective programmes include social skills learning and cognitive models, skills training, differential association and behavioural systems including family therapy.

There has been a disturbing increase in the amount of sex offences (White *et al.*, 1992). In the treatment of sex offenders, behaviour modification techniques for modifying erotic responses and reinforcing appropriate social behaviour have been found to be effective (Bluglass, 1981).

PSYCHOPATHIC OFFENDERS

Psychopathic offenders are the most controversial of client groups. The very existence of psychopathic disorder as one category of mental illness has been debated for years (Chiswick, 1987). According to Holland *et al.* (1980), psychopaths comprise a relatively small percentage of prison inmates; they tend to be more in psychiatric facilities rather than in prisons.

Psychopathic disorder as legally defined depends on abnormal aggression and serious irresponsibility; the disorder is one of behaviour and socialization (Chiswick, 1987). Psychopaths feature in common persistently difficult behaviour (Roth, 1986). It has been found that those persons with a psychopathic disorder released from the special hospitals are more likely than most other groups to commit further offences (Chiswick, 1987).

Psychopathic offenders have not committed their offences in the context of illness. The choice of treatment is not clear and it is difficult to establish whether relevant change has occurred (Dell *et al.*, 1987). Black (1984) suggests that it is necessary to look at the mix of individual and environmental causes when treating psychopaths and to provide treatment programmes to modify behaviour. Roth (1986) suggests that treatment should be self-sought by the individual and that the decision for treatment have no direct relationship with parole decisions or release from the institution.

What to do about psychopaths is a question that has been frequently raised and there appears to be no consensus of opinion. Psychopaths are an extremely difficult management issue and, for this reason, the debate continues as to whether they should be placed in special prisons or special prison units having medical input, regular prisons or secure hospital settings (Roth, 1986).

WOMEN OFFENDERS

In the past, women have represented only a small proportion of the entire prison population when compared to male offenders. Except in the category of violent crimes, the number of arrests of women in all crime categories has increased in recent years (Desmond, 1991; Roundtree *et al.*, 1980; Sobel, 1980). Regardless of the reason for the increase, the fact remains that women prisoners not only have been a relatively forgotten group in the prison system but have been subjected to biased policies and programmes that cause them to experience more physical and mental health problems than do male prisoners (Sobel, 1980).

It has been found that an antisocial personality, inter-personal difficulties, alcoholism, hysteria and drug dependency characterize many female inmates and that they frequently came from poor educational and occupational backgrounds (Martin *et al.*, 1978). An analysis of criminal recidivism disclosed significant relationships to past criminal record, psychiatric diagnoses, education, age, an index crime of robbery, marital status and family history (Martin *et al.*, 1978). Antisocial personality and drug dependence were particularly associated with high rates of re-arrest and re-conviction.

Loneliness is a powerful variable for women inmates and one possibly greatly influencing or affecting health and illness. Many women incarcerated in institutions develop physical symptoms as an indicator of their emotional distress since they cannot express their conflict in other more constructive ways. In a survey of medical complaints, Sobel (1980) found that gynaecological problems, nerves (anxiety), depression, headaches and respiratory infections were the most common complaints. Psychiatric patients in prison tend not to have a higher incidence of psychotic illnesses but that, as a result of imprisonment, there is an increase in the number who had neurotic symptoms (Wilfley *et al.*, 1986).

Dell and associates (1993a) found that of the group of psychotic women they studied in prison, most had a previous conviction, with theft being the commonest offence. Major violence was not common. They found that prior to deten-tion a large proportion of these women had been living in squats, hostels, rooming houses and the like. In a further study of a non-psychotic population of women in prison, Dell and associates (1993b) found that the typical woman was charged with property offences, had a considerable previous record and was often on drugs.

Anger is a powerful emotion inextricably connected to feelings of powerlessness. When an individual perceives no effective alternatives to a situation and experiences frustration, interference, manipulation, exploitation, unfair criticism or humiliation, then anger is often the result.

This anger may go in two main directions: aggression or suppression. Characteristics, experiences and behaviour of female offenders before incarceration do affect their prison behaviour (Roundtree *et al.*, 1980). This may result in violent acting-out aggressive behaviour in some cases. On the other hand, it may result in suppression, as many women in our society are socialized to believe that they have no right to be angry. They then are more likely to repress their anger to the point that it becomes uncontrollable, thereby creating both physical and psychological distress (Wilfley *et al.*, 1986).

Women's closed prisons are notorious for the high degree of tension which they generate. Carlen (1985) found that over-rigid discipline leads to both the high degree of tension in women's prisons and to the proportionately higher number of discipline charges levelled against female as compared with male offenders which in turn leads to heightened distress.

According to Burrow (1992), young personality-disordered females were the most prominent group of self-harmers from the hospital population. A number of explanations have been put forward for self-harming behaviour, including deprived socioeconomic circumstances, confinement, boredom and frustration (Burrow, 1992). Additionally, backgrounds of childhood physical or sexual abuse, repeated surgery and trauma have been found to be significant in persons developing self-harming behaviours (Van der Kolk *et al.*, 1991).

When childhood trauma is repeated, borderline clients can develop intractable depressive, psychotic and psychotic-like symptoms (Perry *et al.*, 1990). Borderline clients are profoundly distrustful, frequently re-enact traumatic patterns with others and experience periodic regressions. Perry and associates (1990) suggest that the issue of trauma history must be addressed in psychotherapy.

Treatment of borderline clients is a long and difficult task. Intensive treatment of borderline clients needs to have the stability of the framework of treatment, increased activity by the therapist and tolerance of the client's hostility. Aspects of intensive treatment include making self-destructive behaviours ungratifying, establishing a connection between the client's actions and feelings in the present, blocking acting-out behaviours, focusing early clarifications and interpretations on the here and now and paying careful attention to counter-transference feelings (Waldinger, 1987).

Nahmias and Froehlich (1993) suggest that health professionals have an obligation to understand the developmental and social contexts of the women they treat.

THE ELDERLY OFFENDER

When thinking about the words crime and offenders, most people tend to have the stereotyped image of the young male offender. Research, however, suggests that the numbers of elderly offenders are increasing (Vito and Wilson, 1985).

It has been found that the elderly inmate shows less psychopathology but displays more symptoms of anxiety, despondency, insecurity and inadequacy (Vito and Wilson, 1985). A number of physical and mental changes take place for older individuals. All the mental processes slow down and the time required for adjusting to a new situation is increased; they have less ability to withstand pressure. In addition, the physiological process of ageing results in diminution of reflexes, sensory losses and an increase in chronic disabling conditions.

Various emotional and behavioural reactions occur as people undergo the physiological changes of the ageing process. These reactions include anxiety, frustration, fear, depression, intolerance, stubbornness, loneliness, decreased independence, decreased productivity, low self-esteem and numerous somatic complaints (Shives, 1990). This occurs as part of the ageing process in general. Being institutionalized heightens these reactions.

Loss is a predominant issue for older people. They may experience loss of control over daily routines, loss of roles and identity, confinement and social isolation. In addition, there is always present the inevitability of death (Bailey *et al.*, 1984; Shives, 1990). When elderly people cannot resolve the feelings they are experiencing, they often develop neurotic or psychotic disorders.

The elderly are a high-risk group for committing suicide. Bailey *et al.*, (1984) found that although the elderly account for about 10% of the population, 25% of all suicides are committed by this group of people. Suicide methods used by the elderly are more violent and lethal than in any other age group (Courage *et al.*, 1993). The health professional needs to be alert to any emotional and behavioural changes taking place with the elderly offender.

The elderly have many life issues that need to be addressed: abandonment, dependency, poor health, mortality, loss of purpose, loss of former identity and loss of independence (Courage *et al.*, 1993; Pearlman, 1993). Group psychotherapy enables the elderly to talk about their problems and concerns and has been found to be an effective therapeutic intervention (Pearlman, 1993).

A high proportion of elderly patients confined to mental health institutions suffer from senile brain atrophy. The patient may show confusion, wander around aimlessly, have little emotional control and is often irritable and argumentative with other patients and staff (Bailey *et al.*, 1984).

Elderly persons with mental illnesses present a complex picture. Problems such as dementia, depression, and psychotic disorders are often compounded by non-psychiatric problems. This may include a wide range of things such as health problems of physical disability, difficulties in self-care, altered or stressed support systems, loss of major life roles and a decreasing ability in carrying out basic daily living activities (Trace and Howell, 1991).

Older persons with psychiatric disorders are often at risk of losing their independence at many levels. Detachment and inactivity are often seen. Owing to performance deficits associated with mental illness, for example, changes in memory, perception, energy levels, or co-ordination, older people may develop increased expectations of failure, avoid activities and involvement with others, and thus experience a further decline in their skills.

Persons with chronic mental illness are characteristically dependent individuals who see themselves as ineffective and helpless (Drew, 1991). The fact that they may look and act different often excludes them from the ordinary social interactions that provide opportunities to develop one's social self. Because of diminished mental and emotional resources, they may be unable to establish satisfying connections with others.

Programmes need to be designed to recognize the special needs of the elderly rather than having a programme for the so-called average offender. The elderly present a challenge in programme design since a combination of factors need to be considered – cognitive, physical, socioemotional and environmental.

MENTAL HANDICAP

With mental handicap there is a lack of normal intellectual development resulting in the individual's inability to function fully or adequately in everyday life. Mentally handicapped individuals do not demonstrate only one area of difficulty but manifest an interaction of multiple factors among which are socio-cultural, psychological and physical influences.

A disproportionately high number of individuals with mental handicap are involved in delinquent or criminal activity. They are thought to comprise about 10% of the prison population (Drew *et al.*, 1992). The mentally handicapped person who comes into contact with the criminal justice system is at a definite disadvantage due to the criminal justice system's unfamiliarity with and uncertainty in dealing with mentally handicapped individuals. Rockoff and Hofman (1977) found that mentally handicapped inmates tended to commit more violent crimes than expected and were arrested more frequently than expected.

Mentally handicapped inmates are more easily and more frequently victimized by other inmates. They are the recipients of much verbal and physical abuse. Verbal abuse such as calling the person an 'idiot' is very demeaning and destructive of human worth. The mentally handicapped inmate faces twin problems owing to the fact that they are impaired in social intelligence as well as intellectual functioning. They have more difficulty in understanding institutional rules and regulations and more frequently violate them with subsequent punishment.

Suicide does occur in the mentally handicapped population but, according to Vitiello and Behar (1992), is not frequent. Non-life-threatening, self injurious behaviours are common with the mentally handicapped patients. The most commonly diagnosed psychiatric disorders among mentally handicapped patients is that of disruptive behaviour disorders, for example, temper tantrums and inappropriate acts. Adjustment disorders occur frequently as a result of their impaired adaptability to novel stressors.

Depending upon the level of mental handicap, there will be some degree of difficulty in communication. Most mentally handicapped patients operate on a concrete level with poor verbal expression and comprehension. They are often easily distracted which affects their ability to concentrate on a particular task. Difficulties with task completion can lead to feelings of frustration and anger (Bailey *et al.*, 1984).

Programmes need to be designed that take into account the level of functioning of the mentally handicapped patient. Programmes should be structured, have clear directions and instructions for the group members and should probably focus on basic living skills tasks plus an awareness of how to communicate needs more appropriately.

ACQUIRED IMMUNE DEFICIENCY SYNDROME (AIDS)

The AIDS virus is carried in the blood and blood-related products, especially semen. It is mostly contagious through intimate sexual contact or by the sharing of needles by IV drug users. The AIDS virus affects the person's immune system, leading to either secondary infections or malignant cancer. All of the AIDS diseases have extremely painful, debilitating and devastating physical and psychological effects (Southwell, 1990).

The physical symptoms of AIDS may include nausea and vomiting, chronic headaches, weight loss, fatigue, painful mouth infections, hypotension, central nervous system dysfunction and psycho-motor retardation and severe respiratory distress (Southwell, 1990).

The person with AIDS may experience a number of emotional and social reactions including a loss of self-esteem, changes in body image, feelings of isolation and stigmatization, an overwhelming sense of hopelessness and a sense of loss of control over their lives. In addition, they may experience anxiety, guilt, anger, depression and express suicidal ideation (Southwell, 1990).

Functional impairment experienced by the person with AIDS can be extensive owing to the complex nature of the interaction between the physical, neurological, psychological and social effects of the disease. This causes impairment in the ability to perform tasks, attend to life roles, and carry out basic daily living tasks, for example, self-care and mobility (Loveland, 1992).

AIDS has presented several administrative and clinical management issues in correctional facilities as well as financial, medical, and legal issues. As time progresses AIDS cases in correctional facilities have increased (Schindler, 1990). Incidence rates are higher in the correctional system than in the general population due to the concentration of persons with high-risk behaviours, especially IV drug users.

The complex issue of HIV transmission in correctional facilities sparks much controversy since it alludes to security difficulties in the institutions. HIV infection can be transmitted through sexual activity and IV drug use.

Tattooing and sharing of razors are common in some correctional facilities and these activities can expose an inmate to the HIV virus. Since a common behaviour among inmates is assaultiveness towards fellow inmates and staff, the risks of contracting the virus from an inmate who is HIV positive is a concern among staff members (Schindler, 1990).

It is important for the health care professional to have a comprehensive knowledge of AIDS conditions and possible presentations. This knowledge will affect the nature of assessments and treatment strategies that are employed. The client's condition will fluctuate and change in the course of the illness and the therapist should be alert to the changing needs of the person.

OFFENDERS REQUIRING AFTERCARE

Mentally ill offenders require skilled support and a high level of supervision and aftercare by health professionals on their release to the community (Chaloner and Kinsella, 1992; Parry, 1991). Many of these clients require more intensive support than that typically offered at out-patient clinics.

For clients who have spent a long time in institutions, either prisons or forensic psychiatric facilities, the transition to the community is particularly difficult. Major issues centre around problems associated with daily living, for example, finding housing, form filling, coping with bills, loneliness, poor diet and lack of self-care (Chaloner and Kinsella, 1992; Parry, 1991).

Treatment for this group of clients should have a strong component of supportive psychotherapy and a practical approach to problem-solving in daily living activities.

SUMMARY

This chapter has looked at the characteristics of some of the clients typically seen in forensic facilities. There is a complex interaction between mental health, criminality, and effects of the environment. The health professional needs to be alert to the impact of the environment, mental illness and the special needs of the clients in designing treatment programmes.

REFERENCES

Bailey, D., Cooper, S. and Bailey, D. (1984) *Therapeutic Approaches to the Care of the Mentally Ill*, 2nd edn, F.A. Davis Company, Philadelphia, pp. 247–54.

Benezech, M., Bourgeois, M. and Yesavage, J. (1980) Violence in the mentally ill. *Journal of Nervous and Mental Disease*, **168**, 698–700.

Black, T. (1984) Treatment in maximum security settings, in *Mentally Abnormal Offenders*, (eds M. Craft, and A. Craft), Ballière Tindall, London, pp. 350–83.

Bluglass, R. (1981) Advances in forensic psychiatry in England and Wales. *International Journal of Law and Psychiatry*, **4**, 199–212.

Burrow, S. (1992) The deliberate self-harming behaviour of patients within a British special hospital. *Journal of Advanced Nursing*, **17**, 138–48.

Carlen, P. (1985) Law, psychiatry, and women's imprisonment: A sociological view. *British Journal of Psychiatry*, **146**, 618–21.

Chalnor, C. and Kinsella, C. (1992) Care with conviction. *Nursing Times*, **88**, 50–2.

Chiswick, D. (1987) Managing psychopathic offenders: A problem that will not go away. *British Medical Journal*, **295** 159–60.

Courage, M., Godbey, K., Ingram, D. *et al.* (1993) Suicide in the elderly: Staying in Control. *Journal of Psychosocial Nursing*, **31**, 26–31.

Dell, S., Robertson, G., James, K. *et al.* (1993a) Remands and psychiatric assessments in Holloway prison I: The psychotic population. *British Journal of Psychiatry*, **163**, 634–40.

Dell, S., Robertson, G., James, K. *et al.* (1993b) Remands and psychiatric assessments in Holloway prison II: The non-psychotic population. *British Journal of Psychiatry*, **163**, 640–4.

Dell, S., Robertson, G. and Parker, E. (1987) Detention in Broadmoor: Factors in length of stay. *British Journal of Psychiatry*, **150**, 824–7.

Desmond, A. (1991) The relationship between loneliness and social interaction in women prisoners. *Journal of Psychosocial Nursing*, **29**, 5–10.

Dixon, B. and Polaschek, D. (1992) Development and evaluation of a treatment programme for violent offenders, Conference proceedings, *Progress in Forensic Psychiatry*, Auckland, pp. 94–100.

Drew, N. (1991) Combating the social isolation of chronic mental illness. *Journal of Psychosocial Nursing*, **29**, 14–7.

Drew, C., Logan, D. and Hardman, M. (1992) *Retardation: A Life Cycle Approach*, 5th edn, Macmillan Publishing Company, New York.

Hartstone, E. and Cocozza, J. (1983) Violent youth: The impact of mental health treatment. *International Journal of Law and Psychiatry*, **6**, 207–24.

Holland, T., Levi, M. and Watson, C. (1980) Personality patterns among hospitalized vs incarcerated psychopaths. *Journal of Clinical Psychology*, **36**, 826–32.

Johnson, J. (1986) Wellness and occupational therapy. *American Journal of Occupational Therapy*, **40**, 753–8.

Loveland, J. (1992) Occupational therapy, in *AIDS in Australia*, (eds E. Timewell and D. Plummer), Prentice Hall, Englewood Cliffs, New Jersey, pp. 304–23.

Martin, R., Cloniger, C. and Guze, S. (1978) Female criminality and the prediction of recidivism. *Archives of General Psychiatry*, **35**, 207–14.

Nahmias, R. and Froelich, J. (1993) Women's mental health: Implications for occupational therapy. *American Journal of Occupational Therapy*, **47**, 35–41.

Parry, J. (1991) Community care for mentally ill offenders. *Nursing Standard*, **5**, 29–33.

Pearlman, I. (1993) Group psychotherapy with the elderly. *Journal of Psychosocial Nursing*, **31**, 7–10.

Perry, J., Herman, J., Van der Volk, B. *et al.*, (1990) Psychotherapy and psychological trauma in borderline personality disorder. *Psychiatric Annals*, **20**, 33–43.

Robertson, G. (1988) Arrest patterns among mentally disordered offenders. *British Journal of Psychiatry*, **153**, 313–6.

Rockoff, E. and Hofman, R. (1977) The normal and the retarded offender: Some characteristic distinctions. *International Journal of Offender Therapy and Comparative Criminology*, **21**, 52–6.

Roth, L. (1986) Correctional psychiatry, in *Forensic Psychiatry and Psychology, Perspectives and Standards for Interdisciplinary Practice*, (eds W. Curran, A. McGarry, and S. Shah), F.A. Davis Company, Philadelphia, pp. 429–68.

Roundtree, G., Mohan, B. and Mahaffey, L. (1980) Determinants of female aggression: A study of a prison population. *International Journal of Offender Therapy and Comparative Criminology*, **24**, 260–69.

Schindler, V. (1990) AIDS in a correctional setting. *Occupational Therapy in Health Care*, **7**, 171–83.

Shives, L. (1990) Psychosocial aspects of ageing, *Basic Concepts of Psychiatric-Mental Health Nursing*, 2nd edn, (ed. L. Shives), J.B. Lippincott Company, Philadelphia, pp. 591–610.

Sobel, S. (1980) Women in prison: Sexism behind bars. *Professional Psychology*, **11**, 331–8.

Southwell, R. (1990) Coping with acquired immune deficiency syndrome (AIDS), in *Basic Concepts of Psychiatric-Mental Health Nursing*, 2nd edn, (ed. L. Shives), J.B. Lippincott Company, Philadelphia, pp. 581–9.

Taylor, P. (1985) Motives of offending among violent and psychotic men. *British Journal of Psychiatry*, **147**, 491–8.

Trace, S. and Howell, T. (1991) Occupational therapy in geriatric mental health. *American Journal of Occupational Therapy*, **45**, 833–8.

Tse, S. (1990) Occupational therapy in a forensic psychiatric unit. *New Zealand Journal of Occupational Therapy*, **41**, 18–22.

Van der Kolk, B., Perry, C. and Herman, J. (1991) Childhood origins of self-destructive behaviour. *American Journal of Psychiatry*, **148**, 1665–71.

Vitiello, B. and Behar, D. (1992) Mental retardation and psychiatric illness. *Hospital and Community Psychiatry*, **43**, 494–9.

Vito, G. and Wilson, D. (1985) Forgotten people: Elderly inmates. *Federal Probation*, **49**, 18–24.

Waldinger, R. (1987) Intensive psychodynamic therapy with borderline patients: An overview. *American Journal of Psychiatry*, **144**, 267–74.

White, L., Jennings, I., Shaw, J. *et al.* (1992) Sex offenders and the courts: A review of sex offenders' cases in South Australia and the role of psychological/psychiatric reports. Conference proceedings, *Progress in Forensic Psychiatry*, Auckland, pp. 129–33.

Wilfley, D., Rodon, C. and Anderson, W. (1986) Angry women offenders: Case study of a group. *International Journal of Offender Therapy and Comparative Criminology*, **30**, 41–51.

Zitrin, A., Hardesty, A., Burdock, E. *et al.* (1976) Crime and violence among mental patients. *American Journal of Psychiatry*, **133**, 142–9.

4

The environment

The environment influences the attitudes and behaviours of individuals. This not only holds true for the clients but for the people who work there. Institutional settings exert a powerful effect in a number of ways: the level of security, the expectation of control, isolation, fear of violence and so on. It is important for staff working in these types of settings to have some understanding of the dynamics of institutional settings for both clients and for staff. By understanding this process more fully, staff are better equipped to deal with specific issues such as establishing the therapeutic environment, handling violence, improving the work environment, and to learn more effective coping strategies.

This chapter aims to look at a number of issues that confront staff in an institutional setting and ways in which the working environment can be made less stressful. This chapter explores:

- violence in institutions
- handling the violent client
- creating the therapeutic environment
- staff issues.

VIOLENCE IN INSTITUTIONS

A number of studies have been conducted looking at clients' violence in various institutional settings. The incidence of violent behaviour has increased in recent years and is a growing concern for people (Davis and Boster, 1988). Although, on the whole the violence is not serious, at times it does have tragic consequences (Mawson, 1990; Whitman *et al.*, 1976). For people working in these settings, there is always present the concern among staff members that clients may suddenly become assaultive and generally destructive (Levy and Hartocollis, 1976).

A number of mentally ill people behave in a violent and frightening manner because of the interaction between their illness and their personality. However, it is not just the type of client seen in secure settings that are the cause of violence taking place.

Many of the circumstances that precede violence are well-established, such as overcrowding and the congregation of clients at certain times, for example, meal times (Mawson, 1990). Boredom and feeling helpless, anger about tension on the ward or about unwanted medication, insufficient therapeutic activity, arguments, invasion of personal space, lack of privacy, provocation, the institutional milieu and staff attitude are all additional factors that precipitate violence (Levy and Hartocollis, 1976; Mawson, 1990; Whitehead, 1975).

Crowded conditions in the institutional setting and shortage of personnel mean that relatively few clients can get the attention they need from busy staff members (Levy and Hartocollis, 1976). Some clients are likely to act-out to get attention, or others might do so as a result of their emotional needs not being met. Certain disturbed clients are noted, as a result of their behaviour, to increase the likelihood of their being victimized or alternatively may act as a catalyst elsewhere within the ward (Mawson, 1990).

Clients more likely to act violently have psychotic conditions, in particular schizophrenia, i.e. paranoid schizophrenia or other psychotic disorders involving paranoid delusions; organic brain-disordered or dementia clients; substance abuse; epilepsy and temporal lobe abnormalities. Blair and New (1991) suggest that it is the severity of the pathology that is the predisposition to violence, making diagnosis only indicative at best.

Interestingly, a history of assault in the community is not a good indicator of assault in a treatment setting. A history of assault in a treatment setting, instead, is by far the most widely recognized risk factor for assault (Blair and New, 1991). This means that one has to look at the nature and structure of service and the implications this has for violent behaviour.

Violence on the whole is the product of a hospital's social structure and process. Violence is inherent in coercive, regimental organizations where people feel themselves to be denied the normal social behaviours and requirements of daily living (Conference Report, 1978). This also applies to prison violence. Recent research on prison violence has implicated several causative factors such as the violent nature of prison inmates and prison control systems, the lack of prison recreational, educational, and therapeutic services for inmates, institutional crowding and architectural design (Shoemaker and Hillery, 1980).

An authoritarian system, particularly if illness is viewed from the medical model, leads to isolation of staff from clients. There is then the acceptance that assaultive behaviour is viewed as a symptom of the illness (Blair and New, 1991; Mawson, 1990). Those staff who are rigid, intolerant, and oppressive greatly influence the milieu. Whitehead (1975) suggests that fear and ignorance on the part of staff are contributing factors for them behaving in this manner. Data gathered indicates that responses to a perceived threat are stereotyped and instantaneous (Whitman *et al.*, 1976).

A primary factor of provocation is that of limit setting. Clients are often very resistive to having limits placed on them, and many injuries occur when staff try and enforce the limits. Most of the injuries are sustained during the day when more demands are made on the clients (Ghaziuddin and Ghaziuddin, 1992).

Staff attitude is another issue provocation. Blair and New (1991) found that assaulted staff generally report they don't like the client who assaulted them. They suggest that perhaps their animosity is projected onto the client. Arrogant, bossy staff, being pushed around, and having one's opinions and emotional needs disregarded is more than enough to provoke clients (Whitehead, 1975).

Alternatively, feelings of inadequacy concerning the staff's ability to handle a difficult situation, when accompanied by frustration and anger, can increase the chances of driving a disturbed client to violence. Von Holden (1980) suggests that one of the biggest problems in the forensic area has been to attract high-quality staff that feel confident in dealing with the types of issues that may arise.

Other issues to look at involve inadequate training, understaffing the service and the poor communication or underinvolvement of medical staff which also play their part in the existence of violence in institutions (Mawson, 1990).

Madden *et al.* (1976) looked at whether psychiatrists might overtly or covertly provoke the violent behaviour of their clients. They found that psychiatrists who had been assaulted varied considerably in age and level of experience. The issues that triggered these assaults were reported as refusing to meet a client's request, forcing a client to take medication, setting either too many or too few limits and the way material was dealt with in therapy.

Levy and Hartocollis (1976) in their research found that the overemphasis in the use of male nursing aides is more likely to lead to violence than prevent it. They suggest that having the expectation of violence and destructive behaviour may constitute a self-fulfilling prophecy.

Likewise, Blair and New (1991) found that locked units and severe structure may increase the risk for assaultive behaviour by implying that abnormal or disturbed behaviour is acceptable in such settings – assaults become an expected occurrence. Unfortunately in these settings, all too often job performance is defined as keeping the clients under control with the use of medication, seclusion and restraints, all of which are intrusive and provocative.

Blair and New (1991) found that nursing assistants and student nurses have a higher incidence of assault which they suggest is because they lack the skills, training and experience of more mature staff members.

Violence threatens the welfare of clients, visitors, and staff. It is, therefore, important to understand and identify the various risk factors associated with violence, and to develop skills to be more personally effective. It is felt that a high staff:client ratio is essential in being able to provide meaningful treatment for the violent mentally ill (Von Holden, 1980).

Whitehead (1979) suggests that the establishment of more humane and less depersonalized regimes is important in reducing the incidences of violence. An essential factor in being able to provide a more therapeutic environment relates to staff attitude and training.

It is of advantage to both clients and staff to be in a more therapeutic environment. A rigid, regimented environment which influences the number of assaults that take place has far-reaching consequences. Assaults by clients on staff may involve injury, lost time, high stress, job dissatisfaction and subsequent psychological effects. This unpleasant working environment has deleterious effects on the functioning of both clients and staff (Beck *et al.*, 1991; Blair and New, 1991). This then frequently leads to high staff turnover which is disruptive to the smooth running of therapy programmes. There is also a reluctance of staff to take a job in an environment which they perceive to be violent.

HANDLING THE VIOLENT CLIENT

Anger may be expressed in a variety of ways starting from verbal aggression (verbal abuse, sarcasm, demands) at one end to physical violence at the other (Gluck, 1981; Morrison, 1992). If the staff responds in a non-therapeutic manner this is more likely to intensify rather than resolve anger. Some examples of this might include:

- becoming defensive or making excuses
- minimizing the situation
- ignoring the client's feelings and concerns
- responding angrily to the client and
- antagonizing or humiliating the client.

It is well understood that it is not easy for staff to work with clients who are angry and potentially violent. Staff are often under a good deal of stress on an ongoing basis. Working in an atmosphere in which there is a threat of personal attack is likely to cause anxiety and stress reactions (Burnard, 1991). It is important, therefore, for staff to be educated about violence, to be provided with support and to learn methods of intervention to be more effective (Stevenson, 1991).

Education about violence

Violence is part of a process – there is progression from relative calm to increasing agitation to acting-out behaviour. Staff need to be able to accurately assess the client's immediate potential for violence and to decide what is the most appropriate method of dealing with the situation. There are a number of options that the staff may choose to employ. These include:

- administer medication
- putting client in seclusion room
- physical restraint
- interruption of the interaction
- non-verbal minimization of self as a threat and
- therapeutic communication.

To be more effective and to feel more confident in this type of high-security setting, there are a number of general issues concerning personal development, communication skills and safety considerations that can be looked at. The therapeutic use of self and knowledge of preventative measures are the first steps in feeling more confident in one's ability to handle the situation.

Identifying personal stressors

It is important for staff to be able to focus their full attention on their job. If staff allow stressors to influence their ability to carry out their work effectively, the situation becomes compounded. Staff need to be able to identify the stressors they are experiencing and take steps to manage them. This might include going to the supervisor, talking to colleagues, having some time out, and ongoing education in order to increase self confidence and skills in being able to handle clients effectively.

Knowing one's capabilities

In order to be more effective in working with clients, it is necessary for staff to look at their style of interaction with clients and to assess the quality of this interaction. It is important for staff to have supervision and be open to feedback about the therapeutic interventions they make.

Increasing understanding of violent clients

Role-playing techniques in which one staff takes the part of an assaultive client, and the other the therapist, is a useful way to gain insights into the feelings and impulses of such clients and how they might respond to different therapeutic interventions.

Knowing the clients

It is important to get to know all the clients on the ward, to spend time talking to them and to let them know that you are approachable. By doing so, it is easier to try to identify the types of stressors that may set individual clients on a cycle of aggression. It is necessary to be perceptive to any changes in behaviour that may signal that all is not well with the client, for example, pacing, raised voice, staring at a person, clenched fist, rigid posture. Intervention begins by finding out what the client feels is needed. At this stage one can attempt to get the client to a quiet place, acknowledge their feelings, and to express willingness to listen.

Therapeutic communication

Potential problems can be more effectively dealt with by practising the skills of therapeutic communication. Giving an understanding response reflects the client's feelings. This then means that the client's feelings have been validated. An understanding response redirects the focus back to the client which helps the client to recognize their anger, and enables the therapist to try and help the client work through this anger.

The listener shows understanding and acceptance by restating the feeling and content of what the client has communicated. The feeling words are focused on, the general content of the message is noted and body language observed. Being empathic means seeing the situation from the client's eyes. To do this ask yourself: 'What would I be feeling if I was having that experience?' By being understanding, the staff conveys to clients that their feelings matter, that they are being listened to, and that a problem exists. This then enables clients to explore what is the problem and work towards taking action to solve the problem.

There should be congruence between verbal and non-verbal communication. Body language should give clients the same message as what the staff is saying. Staff need to be able to convey that they are calm, caring, receptive, and non-threatening.

Personal space

Clients require adequate personal space. Having their personal space invaded is intrusive and likely to provoke an aggressive response. There are a number of basic things to remember: don't stand over or walk right up behind the client; don't touch a client unless you know how they will view this, as any move towards the client might be interpreted as threatening; and do not stand directly in front of a client.

Communicating with the client

It is important not to take client's swearing personally; don't swear at the patient or over-react by being punitive, accusatory, or challenging. Power struggles will ensue if one attempts to argue with the client. Staff should bear in mind the advantages of:

- speaking calmly to the client;
- using open-ended sentences to promote conversation rather than yes/no responses;
- encouraging the client to take responsibility for their feelings and actions;
- discussing options with the client;
- encouraging the client to make a choice;
- being open with the client – don't say you will do something for them and then not do it;
- always being consistent with limit setting, and
- not confronting the client.

Safety factors

Talk to clients in a quiet area but one that is visible to other staff members. Don't block doorways or make the client feel hemmed in. Being visible adds to the safety of both staff and client. It is important that other staff members know where you are and whom you have with you and for how long you will be seeing them. It is best not to get into a lift alone with a potentially violent client or to walk down the stairs in front of the client.

If the facility has regulations about wearing body alarms, make sure that you comply with the regulations, for example, if you see a staff member being attacked, make sure that you sound the alarm before going to their assistance. Other safety precautions include not wearing dangling earrings, necklaces or scarves that might attract a client to grab them.

In many of these secure facilities, there are workshops or activity rooms with a variety of tools or implements that could be used as a weapon. It is usual to keep tools locked away, to count them before and after use and to only have them unlocked while actually using them. If the client seems unsettled, it would be best to have him involved in an activity/project that didn't include sharps. Make sure that there is adequate staff coverage and that staff are aware of any potential trouble spots and know how to respond to the situation.

CREATING THE THERAPEUTIC ENVIRONMENT

For therapy to take place that is meaningful for the client, a therapeutic environment needs to be created. An essential feature of the therapeutic environment centres around the nature and quality of the relationship that is established between the therapist and client. Research has shown that if the content and quality of the therapist's interventions are poor, then this is detrimental to the patient and may actually harm them (Truax and Carkhuff, 1967). It is important, therefore, that the key objective of early staff-client contact is to establish a relationship which promotes mutual trust (Bailey *et al.*, 1984; Shives, 1990). The therapeutic environment should include:

- being purposeful and planned;
- providing opportunity for exploratory behaviour;
- encouraging social interaction;
- providing a democratic atmosphere;
- maintaining respect for the individual;
- maintaining a positive attitude and encouragement;
- assisting the client in gaining insight into their attitudes and behaviours;
- providing a safe and supportive environment;

- providing opportunity to practice newly acquired skills;
- reinforcing appropriate behaviours, and
- having flexibility and creativity.

In order to develop good communication skills for therapeutic interactions, the therapist should:

- be aware of their own feelings so that this doesn't interfere with their ability to relate to others;
- remember that non-verbal language should reflect what has been said;
- be able to evaluate their own actions and responses;
- be willing to have supervision and listen to feedback;
- feel secure in relating to others, and
- be aware of the importance of showing the client empathy, respect, and genuineness.

Ivey *et al.* (1987) suggest that since nowadays therapists end up dealing with a variety of clients from diverse cultures, a three-step dialectical model of empathy may be useful to consider. They state that this provides a framework for balancing the uniqueness of the individual with the therapist's knowledge and with that of theoretical orientation. This model is outlined as follows:

- Listen to and observe the client and his response.
- Take your response from the client's main words. When in doubt about what is being said use the attending and listening skills.
- Check out your intervention by asking: 'How does that sound?' 'Is that close?' or some other similar statement that allows the client to respond to you.

There are a number of basic communication approaches that the therapist can consider utilizing when interacting with clients. These include:

- Don't use technical jargon with the clients, make sure they understand what you are talking about.
- Clarify and restate any information that is given, since both anxiety and their illness make it difficult to concentrate and they may fail to understand what has been said.
- Don't overload the client with information or therapeutic activity, since if acutely unwell, the attention span may be quite limited and they will overreact to too much stimuli.

- Use simple and direct statements to the client; they will lose the point if what is said is too long and complicated.
- Be specific in what is being communicated and don't make vague generalizations.
- Avoid using discriminatory or emotionally charged words.
- Respond to both the feeling and content of what the client is saying; this validates the person's feelings and experience.
- Focus on the here and now in order to help clients deal with what are the real problems, rather than avoiding them.
- Show that you are attending to the client, for example, eye contact, leaning slightly towards them, responding at appropriate intervals.
- Don't tell the client what the problem is – have the client tell their own story and identify what the problems are as they see them.

An additional part of the communication process involves ethical issues which are essential to address. This includes:

- informing the client that confidentiality will be maintained except if the information may be harmful to others, himself, or he refuses to comply with treatment;
- informing clients of their rights, and
- informing clients of the various treatment methods and procedures.

Shives (1990) suggests that there are three phases of the therapeutic relationship which he identifies as the initiating phase, the working phase, and the terminating phase.

In the initiating phase the therapist gets to know the client. There are a number of basic tasks that need to be carried out including:

- building trust and rapport;
- establishing a therapeutic environment;
- establishing a style of communication that is acceptable to both the client and the therapist, and
- informing the client who you are and what your involvement will be; also establishing the time, place, and duration of each meeting and whether or not it will be time limited.

During the working phase the therapist involves the client in identifying problems and working out steps towards resolution. There are a number of tasks to be carried out in this phase including:

- encouraging the client to be reality-based;
- encouraging the client to develop positive adaptive behaviours;
- promoting the development of positive self-concept;
- encouraging the client to verbalize feelings;
- encouraging the client to identify problem areas;
- encouraging the client to establish realistic goals;
- assisting the client to develop an achievable plan of action;
- encouraging the client to carry out the plan of action; and
- evaluating the plan of action and giving the client feedback regarding their progress.

The therapeutic relationship is terminated when the mutually-agreed goals have been reached. This is the usual case except when the client is transferred or discharged, or the therapist leaves.

In creating and maintaining a therapeutic environment, there are some specific ways the staff can work together to create a better understanding of where they are in client management. Some ways this can be achieved include:

- maintaining current notes on clients;
- having a management plan clearly identified;
- outlining goals of the treatment programme;
- communicating any observed changes in the client to other members of the team as well as charting these changes;
- having regular handover with as many staff attending as possible to talk about what has taken place this shift, and plans for the next shift, making sure that all staff know if anything significant has happened;
- keeping a communication book where staff can write down messages that need to be seen by staff on different shifts, and
- have a board where it can be noted which clients are off the ward, for how long, where and with whom.

As well as the points already mentioned, it is important not to forget the role of informal communication. Staff can share information about clients and how they have handled or dealt with the situations that have arisen. By doing this, the various members of the team can get to know each other better, have increased respect for each other's abilities and can provide support and encouragement for each other.

Jacobs *et al.* (1989) suggest that good communication is essential so that staff relationships won't deteriorate. When staff become over-anxious, and trust and support are not developed, ultimately the effectiveness and efficiency of the team will decline.

Additional ways of looking at the development and maintenance of a therapeutic environment include having an emphasis on quality assurance, measures of outcome and client satisfaction.

Quality assurance involves setting standards, examining processes and measuring outcome (Ellis, 1988; Roberts, 1992). Quality assurance attempts to evaluate a programme's ability to meet its goals. The types of methods used to do this might include: patient chart reviews, audits, peer observations, client surveys. By having quality assurance measures in place, staff will actually know with some precision that the objectives which have been established have standards, criteria and levels which can be measured. Procedures are established that staff can follow to ensure that these levels are being met.

Reviewing the quality assurance programme enables staff to identify problems and propose changes. They can then put in place a quality improvement programme which is an ongoing process, whereby staff continually work towards trying to bring about changes and improvement in the service being offered.

Austin and Clark (1993) suggest that measures of outcome are essential in a health care system to enable monitoring of the service provided and establish the basis for service review and continued development.

Measures of outcome indicate the process of client improvement and achievement of treatment goals. The question that is asked is: 'Is what we are doing effective?' Staff need to know that the provision of service has predicted outcomes.

Nowadays, outcomes are being increasingly looked at in regards to funding and staffing. The responsibility lies with the facility and the service to show that what they do actually makes a significant difference to the client's well-being.

One way that can be utilized to look at how the client views the service is to conduct a well-designed and thought-out client satisfaction survey. Client satisfaction surveys can then help health care managers to improve the quality of their clinical and administrative duties.

Strasser and Davis (1991) suggest that client satisfaction data can be used to:

- make staff accountable for their own high-quality job performance
- help staff identify ways to improve their performance
- help staff identify what they are doing well and to receive acknowledgement for this and
- help improve the quality of care that is delivered.

Staff require clearly identified goals in the setting where they work. They need to know in which direction they are headed since it helps them to prioritize their activities and to think strategically. Strasser and Davis (1991) claim that one of the most potent forces that can pull a team together and build team cohesiveness is a set of commonly shared and valued goals. This then increases the team's ability to identify problem areas, take responsibility and work towards implementing workable solutions.

STAFF ISSUES

Burn-out in the workplace is an issue that needs to be addressed. Even though the subject of burn-out has been widely written about in the literature, no single definition of burn-out has emerged as a standard definition (Burnard, 1991; Sullivan, 1989). In general, burn-out appears to be the end result of a series of events or situations that result in the person feeling continuous stress (Gerrard *et al.*, 1980; Jacobs *et al.*, 1989).

It is important to look at the issue of burn-out since it has profound effects both on the individual and on the quality of care that is delivered. People with burn-out tend to become emotionally detached from the clients and begin to treat them in dehumanizing ways thereby becoming less effective on the job.

There are a wide variety of factors that might contribute to staff burn-out. These could include:

- Work overload – Too much to do causes pressure for the person which decreases their competence in carrying out their job.
- Work underload – Too little to do causes boredom and apathy and questioning of what a person is really meant to be doing.
- Work variety – Lack of variety in the type of work activities carried out can lead to frustration and apathy since there is a lack of challenge and underutiliziation of skills and abilities.
- Work isolation – Lack of contact with other health care professionals leads to isolation and a paucity of intellectual stimulation in their job.
- Work significance – Failure to see any results from treatment interventions leads to the belief that their work has little significance and contributes to feelings of lack of success and dissatisfaction.
- Work activity – Low control over work activity, i.e. doing the specified job with little chance to have any input leads to frustration and resentment.
- Work position – Depending on the person's position in the hierarchy, there are differing degrees of staff participation in decision-making; the further down the hierarchy there is little chance for decision-making resulting in reduced autonomy and feelings of helplessness.
- Work efficiency – Some facilities have lack of organizational efficiency which increases staff's frustration when management doesn't seem to be able to get things done, or they are done very slowly, or, if they are done, are done poorly.
- Work role conflict – When the role of the health care worker overlaps with another discipline, this can result in anger and frustration if the person is challenged about their right to carry out their role or are unable to carry out their job, despite seeing themselves as having the knowledge and ability to do so.
- Work social support – People require the support and encouragement of other members of the team; if this is not available for whatever reason, this leads to feelings of alienation.
- Work supervisors – Supervisors who provide poor leadership are a major source of stress for their staff since they fail to provide direction or support.

- Work feedback – Workers require direct and clear information about how they are carrying out their work requirements; this needs to be non-judgemental.
- Work environments – Some work environments are isolated, poorly maintained, have intrusive security measures, lack equipment and services such as libraries, which all contribute towards staff dissatisfaction with their surroundings and their job.

There are a number of strategies which can be put in place to reduce stress on the job. These include:

- training supervisors in management skills and worker relations;
- regular staff appraisals to have feedback about work performance; this requires having clear set goals and objectives with dates for review;
- training new staff to be able to identify the causes and nature of stress and burn-out;
- providing workshops to help staff learn ways of coping with stress;
- forming staff advocacy groups to provide a forum to explore practical problem-solving means of dealing with pertinent issues;
- providing regular supervision, at least on a weekly basis to discuss what has been happening, how it has happened and what needs to be done;
- providing opportunities for on-going education to help staff upgrade their knowledge, skills and abilities;
- having the supervisor be available and approachable for staff members to go to if they have a problem;
- having a system in place that acknowledges staff member's individual achievements;
- establishing good communication links with other members of the team through meetings, charting and on an individual basis;
- giving workshops on varying aspects of the person's job to increase other team members' awareness of the person's role and capabilities;
- developing a support system within the facility and, if in an isolated position, with other professionals in the neighbouring community;

- accepting the fact that it is essential to take a period of 'time out' during the work day;
- learning not to become over-involved in work to the degree that the person takes it home with them;
- learning to be assertive, and say 'no' to things when a person feels that they are being put upon;
- accepting that it is OK not to know everything and that it is important to be able to ask for help when necessary;
- learning to develop positive coping means of dealing with interpersonal stress, for example, desensitization, covert rehearsal, positive self-statements;
- working on building self-esteem and self-confidence in how the person carries out their work; and
- making sure that the person incorporates into their daily life some form of fitness activity; there needs to be a balance in a person's life between work-related activity and activity away from work.

Von Holden (1980) acknowledges what he terms the 'pressure-cooker' tension which characterizes active treatment programmes dealing with the violent mentally ill, and stresses the importance of special seminars and educational programmes to stimulate professional and intellectual growth. It is also suggested that conducting applied research is another way of furthering professional growth and interest in their work for those health care professionals who choose to work with the violent mentally ill.

SUMMARY

This chapter has looked at environmental considerations and the impact this has on the delivery of care. It is suggested that by concentrating on individual skills and abilities, communication skills, awareness of requirements for a therapeutic environment and by learning positive coping strategies that there will be a benefit to both client care and staff satisfaction.

REFERENCES

Austin, C. and Clark, C. (1993) Measures of outcome: For whom? *British Journal of Occupational Therapy*, **56**, 21–4.

Bailey, D., Cooper, S. and Bailey, D. (1984) *Therapeutic Approaches to the Care of the Mentally Ill*, 2nd edn, F.A. Davis Company, Philadelphia.

Beck, N., Menditto, A., Baldwin, L. *et al.* (1991) Reduced frequency of aggressive behaviour in forensic patients in a social learning program. *Hospital and Community Psychiatry*, **42**, 750–2.

Blair, D. and New, S. (1991) Assaultive behavior: Know the risks. *Journal of Psychosocial Nursing*, **29**, 25–30.

Burnard, P. (1991) *Coping with Stress in the Health Professions*, Chapman & Hall, London.

Conference Report (1978) Handling the violent patient in the hospital. *Hospital and Community Psychiatry*, **29**, 463–7.

Davis, D. and Boster, L. (1988) Multifaceted therapeutic interventions with the violent psychiatric inpatient. *Hospital and Community Psychiatry*, **39**, 867–9.

Ellis, R. (1988) (ed.) *Professional Competence and Quality Assurance in the Caring Professions*, Croom Helm, London.

Gerrard, B., Boniface,. W. and Love, B. (1980) *Interpersonal Skills for Health Professionals*, Reston Publishing Company, Inc., Reston, Virginia.

Ghaziuddin, M. and Ghaziuddin, N. (1992) Violence against staff by mentally retarded inpatients. *Hospital and Community Psychiatry*, **43**, 503–4.

Gluck, M. (1981) Learning a therapeutic verbal response to anger. *Journal of Psychiatric Nursing and Mental Health Services*, **19**, 9–12.

Ivey, A., Ivey, M. and Simek-Downing, L. (1987) *Counseling and Psychotherapy. Integrating Skills, Theory, and Practice*, 2nd edn, Allyn and Bacon, Boston.

Jacobs, P., Crichton, E. and Visotina, M. (1989) *Practical Approaches to Mental Health Care*, Macmillan, Melbourne.

Levy, P. and Hartocollis, P. (1976) Nursing aides and patient violence. *American Journal of Psychiatry*, **133**, 429–31.

Madden, D., Lion, J. and Penna, M. (1976) Assaults on psychiatrists by patients. *American Journal of Psychiatry*, **133**, 422–5.

Mawson, D. (1990) Violence in hospital, in *Principles and Practice of Forensic Psychiatry*, (eds R. Bluglass and P. Bowden), Churchill Livingstone, London, pp. 641–8.

Morrison, E. (1992) A hierarchy of aggressive and violent behaviors among psychiatric inpatients. *Hospital and Community Psychiatry*, **43**, 505–6.

Roberts, A. (1992) Who owns quality in the occupational therapy profession and how do we assure it? *British Journal of Occupational Therapy*, **55**, 4–6.

Shives, L. (1990) *Basic Concepts of Psychiatric – Mental Health Nursing*, 2nd edn, J.B. Lippincott Company, Philadelphia.

Shoemaker, D. and Hillery, G. (1980) Violence and commitment in custodial settings. *Criminology*, **18**, 94–102.

Stevenson, S. (1991) Heading off violence with verbal de-escalation. *Journal of Psychosocial Nursing*, **29**, 6–10.

Strasser, S. and Davis, R. (1991) *Measuring Patient Satisfaction for Improved Patient Services,* Health Administration Press, Ann Arbor, Michigan.

Sullivan, I. (1989) Burnout – A study of a psychiatric center, in *Professional Burnout in Medicine and the Helping Professions,* (eds D. Wessells, A. Kutscher, I. Seeland *et al.,* Hawthorn Press, New York.

Truax, C. and Carkhuff, R. (1967) *Toward Effective Counseling and Psychotherapy: Training and Practice,* Aldine, Chicago.

Von Holden, M. (1980) An open-system approach to the mental health treatment of violent offenders. *Psychiatric Quarterly,* **52,** 132–43.

Whitehead, J. (1975) Violence in institutions. *International Journal of Offender Therapy and Comparative Criminology,* **19,** 87–9.

Whitehead, J. (1979) Violence in mental hospitals and prisons. *International Journal of Offender Therapy and Comparative Criminology,* **23,** 21–4.

Whitman, R., Armao, B. and Dent, O. (1976) Assault on the therapist. *American Journal of Psychiatry,* **133,** 426–31.

5

Assessment

Competent assessment is critical since the results of assessment determine recommendations, treatment planning and ongoing levels of client performance. Treatment planning itself is affected by legal charges and constraints of the legal system. The therapist needs to know the legal status of the individual being referred for assessment and the purpose of the assessment. The legal framework demands a high degree of accountability on the part of the therapist. All results of the assessments need to be conveyed to the referring/treating doctor and to other members of the team so that this information is incorporated into providing an overall picture of the client.

This chapter aims to look at the process of assessment and the elements it contains. A number of steps should be followed that involve the collection of data which is documented in a way that is meaningful, incorporating recommendations, the setting of treatment objectives and the provision for ongoing assessment if required. The goal, then, of assessment is the recording, analysis and interpretation of the problems that were presented. This chapter explores:

- who is involved in assessment
- establishing the therapeutic relationship
- the interview
- investigating other sources of information
- assessment
- conclusions and recommendations
- documentation and
- evaluation.

WHO IS INVOLVED IN ASSESSMENT?

In general, two different types of assessments are conducted. One concerns court reports, the other recommendations relating to treatment in the various forensic facilities.

According to West (1983), assessments of offenders are made in order to help decide the disposal of the offender by the courts at the time of the trial, to guide the allocation of offenders to different institutions while in custody and to assist in the decision to grant early release on parole. Psychiatric reports, which are usually prepared by the prison medical service, and social inquiry reports, prepared by the probation service, are used extensively by the courts.

When psychiatrists are required to advise the courts on medical diagnosis, prognosis or treatment they are called to do so as expert witnesses. What this means is that they must put forth an expert opinion about the effects of the illness in this particular instance. In general, psychiatrists, as part of their testimony, quote test results that are contained in the report rather than calling for other kinds of experts to do so.

Overall then it is more usual for psychiatrists, probation officers and psychologists to be actively involved in presentation of assessments and recommendations to the court. Other health care professionals may at times be called as expert witnesses, but on the whole their role tends to be more focused on what happens to the individual once he or she is admitted to a forensic psychiatric facility.

Assessments are carried out by a variety of disciplines. The purpose of these assessments are threefold:

- an initial assessment to guide treatment planning specific to the needs of the individual.
- to provide ongoing evaluation of the individual's progress in treatment.
- to aid the psychiatrist in providing a comprehensive report about the individual's attitude, behaviour, strengths and weaknesses.

Assessment is seen as the key to treatment effectiveness. It is the foundation for goal setting, the selection of treatment intervention methods and for monitoring of client progress in treatment. The ability to select the correct instruments, to use them effectively, and through the analysis and interpretation of the data, to address the individual's needs and goals meaningfully is the baseline for the provision of effective treatment services.

The referral

Before the process of assessment can begin, the therapist needs to receive a referral from an authorized source according to the policy of the facility. After receiving the referral, the therapist determines the appropriateness and the eligibility of the individual for the treatment programme or service that is offered. The referral source should indicate the reason for referring that individual for assessment and should state general and specific questions which it is hoped will be answered by the assessment.

ESTABLISHING THE THERAPEUTIC RELATIONSHIP

The assessment interview is the first stage of active involvement with the individual. It is at this time that the therapist attempts to initiate an interpersonal therapeutic relationship with the individual.

Even though communication is very much a two-way process, the responsibility for the way communication is carried out rests with the therapist since the therapist is in a helping role. By the time forensic psychiatric clients are being assessed for treatment planning, they will probably have been questioned and interviewed quite a number of times. Despite the fact that an individual may well have been through the system on previous occasions, he or she will still be unsure of what is going to happen in this particular instance as life events to date most likely have been confusing and unrewarding.

Establishing clear communication is an essential first step in the relationship. The individual needs to be informed who the therapist is, their role, and the purpose of the assessment.

There are a number of skills that should be used when engaging in any type of helping relationship. When the individual comes for assessment, the therapist should show that they are attending to the person; this indicates to the person that they have the therapist's full attention. The therapist can ensure that they are in a quiet area, that they resist such distractions as the telephone and other people. The person needs to feel important and that their problems are of interest to the therapist. When interviewing the person the therapist should face them, lean forward slightly and maintain eye contact (Carkhuff, 1980).

The person also needs to know that they are being listened to. The therapist can indicate that they are being attentive by saying 'mmm' or 'yes' at various intervals. It is often the case that people do not always say what is of most significance to them; often there are underlying meanings. Listening closely to how the person says things as well as to the content makes it easier for the therapist to be alert to any underlying concerns that the person might have (Carkhuff, 1980).

It is important to allow the person time to express him or herself and to wait a number of seconds before responding. The therapist should then be able to recall content and paraphrase back to the person what has been expressed (Carkhuff, 1980).

Once the person has explored areas of concern, the goal and the plan of action must be personalized. Personalizing means that the problem, the goal and the plan are personally relevant and meaningful to the individual (Carkhuff, 1980).

Initiating goals for the individual should be a collaborative effort. If the person feels that the goals are not relevant and are not self-imposed, it is unlikely they will have any investment in working towards achieving these goals. Independence should be promoted by helping the individual understand their problem and assuming responsibility for working towards their goals (Anthony *et al.*, 1980).

The relationship between the therapist and the client is important in facilitating skills and understanding. In addition to the above-mentioned skills, there are a number of primary conditions for helping. If these are present at a high level a truly therapeutic relationship can be established.

Empathy is present when the therapist shows the ability to understand the world from the client's perspective and to be able to communicate this understanding to the client (Carkhuff, 1980).

Respect is present when the therapist is able to communicate positive concern and valuing of the client as an individual (Carkhuff, 1980).

Genuineness is present when the therapist is able to be open and straightforward in the relationship with the client. The client needs to feel that the therapist can be depended on (Carkhuff, 1980).

THE INTERVIEW

Interviews can be conducted in an unstructured, semi-structured or structured way. The type of interview used will depend to a large extent on the preference of the therapist.

It is usual that demographic data, historical information, current status and the presenting problem are areas that would be covered in the interview. Emphasis may be placed on one specific area, for example, on work attitude, aptitude and skills if the referral had requested a vocational assessment.

In general the following will be covered:

a. demographic data – name, age, address, contact phone number, schooling, employment, etc.
b. historical information – developmental, family/social environment, medical, legal.
c. current status and presenting problem – the client describes what has taken place and what they identify as problem areas.

In addition, the therapist will note the client's:

- appearance (neat and tidy, scruffy, etc.)
- cognitive (concentration, insight, judgement)
- mood and affect (appropriateness, level)
- behaviour (appropriateness, type, control)
- perception (awareness of reality)
- thought content (appropriateness, organization) and
- emotional defences (denial, projection).

Therefore to determine the current status and presenting problem, the therapist both questions and observes the client.

An example of a structured interview schedule:

FORENSIC ACTIVITIES OF DAILY LIVING QUESTIONNAIRE

1. Identifying Data:

Name: Unit: D.O.B
Charge: Length of Sentence: Release Date:
Serving Prisoner: Mental Health Act: Other:
Previous Charges: Previous Mental Illness:

2. Educational Background:

Grade completed   Type of school:
Upgrading: What grade:
Attended college: What course:
Attended university: What course:
Training in a trade: What trade:
What educational qualifications received:
What educational plans do you have:

3. Employment Background:

Age when you began full-time employment:
What were you doing:
Approximately how many jobs have you held:
Average length of stay in job:
What types of jobs have you held:
Have you ever been fired:
For what reason:
Do you have many periods when not employed:
For what reason:
Occupation before imprisonment/hospitalization:
Length of stay in that job:
Is that job still available to you:

3a. Job-seeking Skills:

Do you find it difficult in applying for a job:
What are some of the difficulties:

Do you know how to fill out a job application/write up a resumé:

3b. Job Behaviour:

Do you have difficulties getting along with your co-workers:
What types of difficulties:
Do you have difficulties getting along with your boss:
What types of difficulties:
Do you have many absences from work:
For what reason:
Do you have any difficulties in carrying out work requirements:
What difficulties do you experience:
Are you able to get to work on time:
Do you consider yourself to be a good worker:
In what way:

3c. Vocational Plans:

Do you have plans for working:
What type of plans:
Do you have plans for vocational training:
What types of enquiries have you made and to whom:

4. Leisure:

What do you like to do in your leisure time:
How frequently do you carry out your hobbies/leisure-time interests:
Do you mostly spend your leisure-time with family or other people:
Do you like leisure activities that involve other people:
Do you prefer leisure activities that you can do alone:
What leisure interests would you like to be involved in:
Are you familiar with local leisure resources:

5. Personal and Home Management:

Do you take care of your personal hygiene independently:
With whom were you living before imprisonment/hospitalization:
What type of residence:

Where do you plan to go once discharged/released:
Were there any children living at home with you:
Which member of the family takes care of the children's:
hygiene, food requirements, school requirements,
discipline, leisure activities:
How many meals a day do you eat:
Do you eat most of your meals at home or out:
Who does the grocery shopping:
Do you know how to plan a meal:
Do you know how to cook:
Who does the housekeeping:
Who does the laundry/clothing repair:
Who does the basic home repairs, i.e. repairing leaking taps,
fixing a fuse, etc.
Do you have your own bank account:
Can you balance your cheque book with the monthly
statements:
Who handles the family's money (pays the bills, rent,
etc.):
Do you have problems with budgeting:
What types of problems:
Do you have a driver's licence:
Do you have your own means of transportation:
Are you familiar with the local public transportation
system:

6. Social Interaction:

Who do you go to when you wish to talk over a problem
or have something you wish to share with someone:
Do you have many friends:
Are they friends that you've had for a long time:
What sorts of things do you like to do with your friends:
Do you like to spend time with people in a social situation:
Do you make plans for social activities or do you wait for
someone to approach you first:
Do you find it difficult initiating a conversation: Why:
Do you find it difficult to maintain a conversation: Why:
Would you like to change the way in which you relate to
others:
What things would you like to change:

> **7. Personal Qualities:**
>
> What do you consider to be your personal good points:
>
> **8. Personal Goals:**
>
> What would you like most to change about yourself:

Forensic Psychiatry for Health Professionals. Chris Lloyd. Published in 1995 by Chapman & Hall, London. ISBN 0 412 48350 5

INVESTIGATING OTHER SOURCES OF INFORMATION

Data is mainly collected through the interview process and by testing the client, but it may be important to review other sources of information. Depending upon the type of assessment that is required, demographic and properly documented background information give more depth to the overall assessment and aid in the interpretation of the client's current level of functioning.

There are a number of different sources that may be utilized:

- interviews with persons significant to the client, for example, family;
- interviews with other professional groups involved with the client, for example, social services, probation services;
- review of test reports by others, for example, psychological report;
- review of reports by others, for example, social history, psychiatric report, and
- review of past records, although Grisso (1986) cautions the use of these records, especially with clients who have accumulated a lengthy official file through extensive contacts with the criminal justice and mental health systems. He suggests that the competence and care with which they were prepared by past observers (police, court employees, mental health professionals) vary considerably.

ASSESSMENT

Vague and inaccurate assessment leads to vague and imprecise treatment. This is not ethical. Intervention must be based on accurate knowledge of the client's needs and abilities. Assessment is a key to treatment effectiveness (Creek, 1990; Moyer, 1984).

A central element in the assessment process is to observe and test function/performance in addition to discussing it in an interview. The type of assesment(s) used will depend greatly on the reason for referral and the orientation of the therapist. Assessments may be qualitative, that is, informal, unstructured and observational or may be quantitative, that is, has reliability, validity, standardization and test norms.

A key reason for the use of quantitative assessments is that it mitigates subjective, discretionary error and provides opportunity for meaningful comparisons. However, there is much to be said for the more informal and qualitative kinds of evaluation. They can produce in-depth data not possible with more structured instruments (Bowker, 1984).

There are a large number of both qualitative and quantitative measures available for use. They vary from the use of in-house assessments to those which have been widely researched and published.

Tests may utilize a number of different means to elicit information, for example, demographic and archival data, behavioural observation methods, base rate information, projective methods, personality inventories, intelligence tests, neuropsychological assessment and interview guides (Anastasi, 1982; Buros, 1978; Grisso, 1986).

There are many traditional measures that can be applied to assessments in the forensic setting. However, there have been a number of specialized forensic measures developed in recent years, a few examples are as follows:

- Competency Screening Test (Lipsitt *et al.*, 1971)
- Interdisciplinary Fitness Interview (Golding *et al.*, 1984)
- A New Scale of Interrogative Suggestibility (Gudjonsson, 1984)
- Rogers Criminal Responsibility Assessment Scales (Rogers, 1984; Slobogin *et al.*, 1984).

These measures usually provide information concerning characteristics of the person under the conditions that prevailed at the time of the assessment. Additional types of data from other sources will be required to address the wider range of information required.

CONCLUSIONS AND RECOMMENDATIONS

Once the therapist has completed the interview, collected additional information and carried out the assessment(s), it is then time to organize the data and observations to formulate an impression and summary of the problem. A plan of action should then be outlined stating what means would be used to work on the specific problems that were identified. It is at this time, that the therapist in the recommendations may refer the client for further assessment, or for treatment programmes run by co-workers.

DOCUMENTATION

Client's records are legal documents and are open to scrutiny by other health care professionals and the legal system. The onus is on the writer to be accountable for what they have written. It is necessary that the information presented is relevant, focusing on the current area of concern and how this has affected the client's functioning. The contents of the report should be specific and not be vague or make generalizations. Objectivity is essential; the contents should not be influenced by writer bias and speculations.

Documentation should show clearly the assessment, problem areas, goals, the treatment plan and ongoing progress of the client. The record should be able to provide those people reading it with a clear and comprehensive picture about what has been happening with the client.

There are a number of considerations to think about when completing documentation. The report should be:

- concise
- comprehensive
- clear
- factual
- accurate and
- objective.

The written report should be clear and follow a logical progression. Subheadings are useful, for example, reason for referral, demographic data, medical/legal status, family history, social history, type of assessment(s) conducted, major problem areas, goals of therapy, recommendations and treatment plan.

If the report is handwritten, the writing should be legible. The use of whiteout and erasure of notes is unacceptable; if an error has been made a line should be drawn through the error, the written correction inserted above or beside the mistake and then the correction initialled.

The report should use correct grammar and spelling, and inappropriate or excess use of jargon should be avoided. Terminology used should be appropriate for those health care professionals who will be reading it.

At the end of the report the writer should date and sign it, making sure that the writer's name, their designation, and department they represent is clearly specified.

EVALUATION

The key to being able to examine progress lies in the setting of goals at the planning stage. If goals are set which state the criteria for success within a given time, the moment will arrive to decide whether the target has been reached or not. If the goal has been met then this indicates, but does not prove, the effectiveness of treatment. If the goal has not been reached this signals the need to re-examine the methods being used and to adjust the programme, the environment or the style of therapy accordingly.

Ongoing evaluation is important in that it provides information about:

- whether client needs have been met,
- whether progress has been made or
- whether the client has regressed.

The steps involved in evaluating individual progress are:

- State goals in behavioural terms.
- Break goals into small observable steps.
- Develop measurement instruments.
- Collect data.
- Interpret the findings.
- Make recommendations.

The assessment provides a baseline for information about the client's attitude, behaviour and function. It is particularly important to monitor how the client functions in the treatment programmes. Re-evaluation allows the therapist to assess at periodic intervals what has been happening for the client – have the goals been achieved? Do new goals need to be set? Do the goals need to be modified?

SUMMARY

This chapter has looked at the process of assessment and how it can be used to increase treatment effectiveness because the specific needs of the patient will have been identified.

REFERENCES

Anastasi, A. (1982) *Psychological Testing*, Macmillan, New York.

Anthony, W., Pierce, R., Cohen, M. and Cannon, J. (1980) *The Skills of Rehabilitation Programming*, University Park Press, Baltimore.

Bowker, A. (1984) Assessment: The keystone of treatment planning, in *Occupational Therapy Assesssment as the Keystone to Treatment Planning*, (ed. F. Cromwell), The Haworth Press, New York, pp. 25–32.

Brodsky, S. and Smitherman, H. (1983) *Handbook for Scales for Research in Crime and Delinquency*, Plenum , New York.

Buros, D. (1978) (ed) *The Eighth Mental Measurements Yearbook*, Gryphon, Highland Park, New Jersey.

Carkhuff, R. (1980) *The Art of Helping IV*, 4th edn, Human Resources Development Press, Cambridge, Massachusetts.

Creek, J. (1990) Assessment, in *Occupational Therapy and Mental Health*, (ed. J. Creek), Churchill Livingstone, Edinburgh, pp. 63–84.

Golding, S., Roesch, R. and Schreiber, J. (1984) Assessment and conceptualization of competency to stand trial: Preliminary data on the interdisciplinary fitness interview. *Law and Human Behaviour*, **8**, 321.

Grisso, T. (1986) Psychological assessment in legal contexts, in *Forensic Psychiatry and Psychology: Perspectives and Standards for Interdisciplinary Practice*, (eds W. Curran, A. McGarry and S. Shah), F.A. Davis Company, Philadelphia, pp. 103–28.

Gudjonsson, G. (1984) A new scale of interrogative suggestibility. *Personality and Individual Differences*, **5**, 303.

Lipsitt, P., Lelos, D. and McGarry, A. (1971) Competency to stand trial: A screening instrument. *American Journal of Psychiatry*, **128**, 105.

Moyer, E. (1984) A review of initial assessments used by occupational therapists in mental health settings, in *Occupational Therapy Assessment as the Keystone to Treatment Planning*, (ed. F. Cromwell), The Haworth Press, New York, pp. 33–41.

Rogers, R. (1984) *Rogers Criminal Responsibility Assessment Scales,* Psychological Assessment Resources, Odessa, Florida.

Slobogin, C., Melton, D. and Showalter, C. (1984) The feasibility of a brief evaluation of mental state at the time of the offense. *Law and Human Behavior,* **8**, 305.

West, D. (1983) Diagnostic practices in use in the criminal-justice system in England, in *Criminological Diagnosis. An International Perspective, Vol II,* (eds F. Ferracuti and M. Wolfgang), D.C. Heath and Company, Lexington, Massachusetts, pp. 527–41.

RESOURCES

Grisso, T. (1987) *Evaluating Competencies: Forensic Assessment and Instruments,* Plenum, New York.

6

Psychotherapy

INTRODUCTION

Individuals do not lead isolated lives. They need to be able to learn to work and live together to manage their lives effectively both in the institutional setting and in society. When attitudes and behaviours individuals hold do not allow for constructive functioning they may require some help in adjusting their attitudes and behaviours in ways that are more socially acceptable. This chapter aims to look at the use of psychotherapy, and in particular the creative arts therapies, with psychologically disturbed people in the institutional setting. This chapter explores:

- psychotherapy
- creative arts therapies
- treatment planning and
- problems associated with the institutional setting.

A large number of clients who come in for treatment in a forensic psychiatric facility suffer from personality disorders or other forms of chronic neurosis, and are likely to be clients for a few years, maybe 3–5 years. It becomes evident that psychotherapeutic skills are of great importance in this type of setting. Most patients require some form of supportive psychotherapy (Gunn, 1986).

PSYCHOTHERAPY

The origins of psychotherapy can be traced back to the early twentieth century, notably with the practice and work of

Freud. The goal of psychotherapy was the growth, maturation and psychological development of the client. Since that time psychotherapy has undergone many changes. One significant change has been the demand that the therapist have more active participation in the process of psychotherapy (Greben, 1987). Another significant development has been that of the introduction of group psychotherapy (Walton, 1971).

In the past it was not uncommon for clients involved in intensive psychotherapy to have their therapists say virtually nothing. This led to dissatisfaction with the way care was being delivered and to the belief that people have the right to receive care that is directed towards their individual needs.

An important move in this direction was made by Rogers (1957) when he coined the phrase 'the necessary and sufficient conditions for therapeutic personality change' (p. 95). This led to considerable interest in empathy as an essential factor in the psychotherapy process (Carkhuff and Berenson, 1977; Hobson, 1985; Kohut, 1984; Truax and Carkhuff, 1967). What the various psychotherapies have in common is that, regardless of their theoretical orientation, therapists tend to be more effective when they can be empathic. Psychotherapy should be able to instil hope and a sense of direction for clients engaging in it.

Group psychotherapy has been seen as an important technique for treating clients having emotionally determined, abnormal behaviour and personality disorders. In forensic psychiatry, where the client has maladaptive social behaviours, group psychotherapy is probably more advantageous to use than one-to-one psychotherapy. This is because group therapy is seen as being more effective in treating and improving a person's social behaviour.

The rationale for group psychotherapy, according to Walton (1971) is that:

1. desired changes occur more readily in a group than with other psychological treatments;
2. such changes are more enduring, and
3. people treated in groups improve their social relationships.

The team approach

The team composition may vary with the setting and client needs. The team usually consists of representatives from psychiatry, psychology, nursing, social work and occupational therapy. The advent of the team approach has had an impact on the delivery of psychotherapy (Margo and Manring, 1989). Information about individual clients accumulates rapidly and is shared through team meetings. This type of organization affects confidentiality. It is the therapist's responsibility to ensure that the client knows that the team members work together in this manner (Margo and Manring, 1989).

Considerations in Group Psychotherapy

Size of the group

It is generally held that the optimum size for a psychotherapy group is about eight client members together with a facilitator and co-facilitator.

Duration of the group

Open groups are those in which members come and go from the group at different times. Closed groups are those in which all members start treatment at the same time and stay together until the group terminates.

Selection of group members

It is usually best to ensure that the group is balanced regarding sex, age and intelligence, and have a mixed range of diagnoses. No one person in the group should be conspicuously different, for example, the only woman. Referrals should be for those clients that it is thought would benefit from group psychotherapy. People that are paranoid or suspicious are not suitable; those clients who are very anxious or insecure may benefit more from a one-to-one therapeutic relationship before embarking on group therapy.

Arrangements for sessions

Ideally sessions should be from 1-1½ hours, and occur on the same day at the same time. The area for sessions should be quiet and free from distractions. All group members sit in a circle so that everyone is visible to each other. It is the member's individual choice as to where they choose to sit. The usual arrangement for the facilitators is for them to sit across from each other to enable them to be alert to any cues from each other. This also allows them to see the other members of the group – to look at people across from them. They are then able to discuss their perceptions of the clients in the group during an aftergroup debriefing, as well as the effectiveness or otherwise of their interventions.

Communication patterns

In group psychotherapy, talk is in the form of free-floating discussion as opposed to didactic, educational, activity or social groups which, although called group therapy, utilize different procedures. The task for members in group psychotherapy is for them to be self-revealing. They deal primarily with the here and now, that is, the pressing problems and concerns that they are experiencing at a given time. What takes place in the group where all members can witness it and contribute is seen as particularly valuable. It is the network of interactions between group members that is the basis for group psychotherapy. Members of the group should feel safe so that they can reveal material that has been kept private, relate to each other, and to experience a sense of support and of being understood. The group atmosphere encourages open communication of attitudes and feelings; members are encouraged to be themselves. A therapeutic group does not have a set agenda, the material that the individual group members bring to the group is dealt with.

The role of the facilitators

The facilitator assists the interactive processes in the group by not being authoritarian or directive so that a group-centred pattern of communication develops. The facilitator's task is to assist group members to reveal themselves fully thereby enabling them to clarify their inner conflicts. The feelings of individuals need to be validated and interventions made that acknowledge how painful or terrifying that must have been. Other group members may be drawn in to encourage their awareness of the distressed person's need for support and understanding.

The facilitator should:

- Be attentive to the nature of emotion and effort in the group.
- Be aware of the interactive processes in the group.
- Be alert as to when it is appropriate to make an intervention.
- Pay active attention to not only individual members but to group processes.
- Make judgements as to whether or not to influence the situation.
- Make decisions about the type of intervention.
- Suspend judgement.
- Tolerate anxiety.
- Communicate understanding to the client.

In addition, the therapist who is involved in running a psychotherapy group should have:

- adequate theoretical knowledge,
- practical experience,
- on-going supervision and
- the opportunity to discuss with the co-facilitator the nature of the interventions and the process of the group.

Therapeutic empathic communication process

Empathy not only has to be communicated to the patient but it also has to be received. Miller (1989) has provided a conceptual framework for analyzing both empathic successes and failures. Empathic understanding must be used to accept, confirm, and validate the total experience of the other person.

Miller (1989) suggests that the process of therapeutic empathic communication proceeds as a five-stage model. He outlines this as follows:

1. The patient sends both verbal and non-verbal cues about their own inner experience.
2. The therapist receives the cues that have been sent by the patient.
3. The therapist processes the communication.
4. The therapist responds to the patient in a partially accurate way and is conveyed both verbally and non-verbally.

5. The patient receives the empathic message from the therapist and accepts the resulting state.

The advantage of conceptualizing the communication of empathy in psychotherapy is that it:

- allows for increased understanding of the interpersonal empathic communication;
- assists the therapist in evaluating the effect of their own empathic interventions, and
- assists the therapist in making adjustments in their therapeutic technique.

CREATIVE ARTS THERAPIES

The creative arts therapies offer experiences which for many clients will facilitate treatment more effectively than traditional verbal approaches (Blatner, 1991). The arts media focus on various expressive aspects in therapy; aspects that involve other modalities in addition to the verbal modality. The arts media includes drawing, painting, music, dance, movement, drama, writing and poetry (Lusebrink, 1991).

The therapist introduces experiences that lead the client to produce and share more personal and emotionally meaningful material. The arts therapies are effective because they build on strengths and serve as a means of promoting social reinforcement. They encourage clients to take on a more active role in their own treatment. There are a wide range of activities and modes for exploring different aspects of a problem.

Basic dynamics

Involvement

Some clients tend to defend themselves from being involved because they fear exposure and vulnerability. If therapy is to be effective clients need to have involvement; they need to be engaged in the therapeutic process. The arts therapies are less threatening than traditional verbal therapy because clients are able to express themselves in a non-verbal manner. Initially sessions can encourage clients to express themselves in a more general manner. Once they feel safe they can then be helped to express more personal issues.

Directness

Have the clients talk about their work in the present, using 'I' statements in terms of feelings not thoughts.

Concretization

Abstract statements need to be changed into something more concrete. With the arts, the client is making some kind of visual statement, for example, drama where he or she is physically enacting a personally relevant situation.

Disclosure

Disclosure involves sharing with others and bringing half-formed ideas to the forefront. Ideas and feelings expressed in the concretized form of some arts media are shared, and feedback is given from other group members.

Imagery

By concretizing this imaginative work, the arts make it easier for many clients to make use of their imaginative capacities which in turn leads clients to experience their own individuality.

Evaluation

Goldberg *et al.* (1991) felt that scales designed for verbal groups were not sensitive to the non-verbal processes inherent in the creative arts psychotherapy groups. They then developed the Therapist Group Process Rating Scale with items being grouped conceptually into the following categories:

- communication
- concrete, insight-oriented
- supportive, uncovering
- emotional expression/inhibition
- sensory/symbolic/creative engagement and
- creativity.

This then allows therapists to keep an ongoing record of the client's involvement in the creative arts psychotherapeutic process.

A number of different authors have written about the approaches they have taken with the creative arts; a few of these are discussed below.

Art therapy

Laing (1984) suggests that the offender has the opportunity to pour out on paper the pent-up emotions and feelings that they would otherwise be unable to express. This then leads to a positive, creative direction for experiencing creativity, and a new sense of self.

Art therapy groups often use a specified theme or structure to stimulate group learning and discussion. Liebmann (1984) recommends that groupwork can be enhanced by using art for the following reasons: everyone can join in at the same time, at their own level; art is an important avenue of communication and expression when verbalization is difficult; art facilitates creativity, and art products are tangible.

Most art groups follow a similar format:

- Introduction – welcome to the group, introductions to new group members, explaining the structure or guidelines for the group. Then introducing the activity for the session.
- Activity – may be spontaneous, for example, scribble on the paper; may be a set theme, for example, draw what I would like to be doing today; may be semi-specified, draw what you like but only use two colours, or may be interactive, for example, a pair might share painting a common theme or the group may work on a common theme.
- Discussion – the art work is used to stimulate discussion about the theme, feelings and creativity.

The therapist assists the group members to develop a means of self-expression and to cultivate some independence within the hospital setting. Art therapy is also an important adjunct in assisting the individual to experience competence and a sense of mastery by being able to produce a tangible achievement. Additionally, it can be used to foster social interaction when group members share paintings and through discussion of individual paintings and the art therapy session.

Birtchnell (1984) suggests that art and psychotherapy enhance each other in that both are concerned with emotional issues. He thinks that art therapy has a wide scope since it allows clients to create a presentation in concrete form, recreating something that is lost or past, and being able to represent safely in pictorial form that which they find frightening.

Imagery

Lusebrink (1989) stated that imagery plays an important role in both creative thought and expression since it carries intensive affective reactions. Lloyd and Campbell (1986–87) utilized individual art therapy, spontaneous imagery and the scribble technique in particular, in order to increase participation in the more verbal-oriented groups.

Music therapy

Hamer (1991) suggests that music is useful to use with low functioning clients. The goal of music therapy is to activate feelings through musical stimuli and encourage expression to bring about change. Music is used in a therapeutic environment to influence changes in the client's feelings and behaviours, by for example, drawing to music, identifying feelings to different types of music and expressing of anger through song to ventilate feeling.

Feder and Feder (1981) suggest that the socializing function of music seems to be the most important single function in music therapy.

Interpersonal relationships

Music is a non-threatening interaction. Music groups give clients a chance of self-assertion and a sense of belonging to the group which promotes interpersonal co-operation.

Self-development

The client is helped to change old habits, to learn new skills and to substitute appropriate behaviours for the old maladaptive behaviours. In a music therapy programme the individual has the ability to make music, to interact with others and to have their abilities reinforced. There is feedback for the individual on his or her own identity and accomplishments. Encouraging improvisation, spontaneity of playing and expression leads to growing self-esteem and a belief in individuals that they can relate to their environment.

Energy and order

The body tends to automatically respond to music. There exists a relationship between musical structure and natural rhythm.

Dance and movement therapy

According to Feder and Feder (1981), it is much easier for an individual to conceal their feelings and thoughts in verbal communication than it is in movement. Body language is always evident. One can observe physical behaviour, that is, what the body and the parts of the body are doing. Movement and stance reflect not only the personality but the individual's emotional state.

Dance and movement therapy help individuals to gain control over their own bodies and to develop accurate body images; they are able to see themselves in relation to the world outside.

The bulk, of human communication is non-verbal. Movement and dance enlarge the individual's capacity to understand and be understood by others, that is, to interpret more accurately the signals of others.

Clients are helped to express impulses and feelings, for example, dance and movement may be an acceptable medium in which to express feelings of anger or frustration if inhibited in their verbal expression. Movement helps project pre-verbal and undifferentiated feelings into the level of consciousness.

Drama therapy

Melnick (1984) used drama skills and professional theatre techniques to teach basic educational skills to adults while providing a safe and therapeutic setting to work on conflicts and problems.

Schramski and Harvey (1983) found in a review that psychodrama and role-playing have a positive effect on resident institutional and post-institutional adjustment.

Sheppard *et al.* (1990) state that drama therapy assists people by providing a means of creative self-expression, relief from tension, and a chance to socialize. The participants are encouraged to create scenarios, dialogues or monologues about situations in life or fantasy through characterization and gesture.

Bibliotherapy

Goldstein (1990) suggests using reading material for therapeutic purposes. The readings should relate to the client's experience or situation. The process of change is centred not so much in the act of reading as in the guided dialogue about the material. The client's response to the reading material facilitates movement in the therapeutic process. It is essential, therefore, that the reading material must be recommended with care and forethought and that the therapist be totally familiar with the material.

Kohutek (1983) suggests that bibliotherapy appears to be particularly useful in prison populations because of its recommended usage for individuals who are either not motivated adequately for verbal therapy or who may require learning more insight prior to therapy.

Films and literature

Lloyd (1987) describes the use of films and literature based on true stories to facilitate personal emotional disclosures, dilute denial and reduce defensiveness, increase empathy with the victim and explore alternatives to restore the emotional damage and lost trust in the relationship.

Therapeutic correspondence

Rosenberg (1990), in responding to the client's letters, used a format which provided extensive support for any positive behaviours, a problem-solving focus on content issues raised, anticipation of future events, requests for further information and a brief personal comment to provide a basis for the client to extend his self-knowledge and institute change in attitude and behaviour. Gunn and Taylor (1983) stress the need for long-term support. It has been found that as far as offending behaviour is concerned, one of the few factors which has been demonstrated to be effective is a supportive relationship with a friend or professional adviser. A relationship can be preserved often by correspondence as the mentally abnormal offender moves through the system (Gunn and Taylor, 1983).

Poetry

Sluder (1990) suggests that for patients very resistant to using the conventional verbal therapies to make self-disclosures, the use of poetry can be a useful approach. One format can be used: introduce a topic, discuss it briefly, read some poems on the topic, have clients write a poem, and then discuss their writing. This enables clients to get in touch with their feelings about what was happening and to share this with other group members. Lloyd (1987–88) describes using poetry on a set theme to assist offenders to develop empathic concern for others as well as emotional awareness and responsibility for their actions.

Humour

A more recent addition to the creative process is described by Buxman (1991) who looks at how humour is a useful adjunct to communication by breaking down barriers, by making people feel good and by bringing them closer together.

The psychotherapeutic use of humour was found to reassure, to convey information and to release tension, stress and anxiety thereby breaking the stress cycle and helping to build self-esteem (Pasquali, 1990). A variety of methods can be used: joke telling, visualization, poetry, limericks, cartoons, films and drawing to encourage clients to create verbal and visual humour (Mango and Richman, 1990).

TREATMENT PLANNING

Considerations for planning a creative arts session

- Timetable the session – determine how often you see the group and for how long.
- Clients and staff members need to be told where and when – let them know the process, the goals and the objectives.
- Specify the type of space you require and the type of equipment that is necessary for you to run the group.
- Determine who will be the staff in the group, for example, in some settings it is possible to choose a co-leader, in other settings staff allocation to group might be arbitrary.

Preliminaries for running the group

- Know who will be in the group.
- Plan specifically for the group.
- Choose activities that will allow group members to succeed.
- Prepare the other staff for being in the group.
- Make sure all the equipment needed for the group is there.
- Check whether all the clients for the group have arrived.
- What is the mood of the group?

Running the Session

- Introduce self.
- Explain what the group is all about.
- Get to know people in the group – the warm-up could consist of everyone saying their names, sharing information/ feelings, likes/dislikes, their favourite activity and so on.
- Introduce activities in a way people can understand.
- Modify the pace if required; work at the group's pace.
- Always start activity at the beginning.
- Be sensitive to the needs of all the group. Try and meet the individual needs of all people within the group.
- Pay attention to all the observed behaviours of the group.
- End the group on a positive but relaxing note.
- Let the group members know when the next session will be (Warren, 1990).

Evaluating the group

- Review how the group responded to other group members and to the activity.

- Think about how the group made you feel and try and pinpoint a reason for this.
- Assess whether or not you met the goals of the activity.
- Document observations about the clients' involvement and participation.
- Assess whether or not you are on the right track.
- Use a record format to graph the clients' participation.
- Use a satisfaction survey to determine whether or not the creative activities have been felt by the clients to be beneficial.

PARTICIPATION RECORD

Name: _____

Participation options:

1 = no participation

2 = inappropriately participating when prompted

3 = participation but inappropriate

4 = appropriately participating only with prompting

5 = appropriate spontaneous participation

Place a dot in the centre of chosen line and connect to previous dot to make a graph of patient participation.

Date	Group Activity	Therapist	Participation 1 2 3 4 5	Comments

---

Forensic Psychiatry for Health Professionals. Chris Lloyd. Published in 1995 by Chapman & Hall, London. ISBN 0 412 48350 5

CLIENT SATISFACTION SURVEY

Name: _____

In order to run groups that best suit your needs it is important for us to know how you find the group.

In the creative arts group we use activities to help you talk about yourself and to gain support from other group members.

Would you please circle the number that best describes how you feel about the statement.

I find I have things in common with other group members.

1	2	3	4	5
Not at all	Rarely	About half the time	Most of the time	Very much so

I find I can share my problems more freely with other group members.

1	2	3	4	5
Not at all	Rarely	About half the time	Most of the time	Very much so

I find I gain support from other group members.

1	2	3	4	5
Not at all	Rarely	About half the time	Most of the time	Very much so

I find I can talk more freely about myself.

1	2	3	4	5
Not at all	Rarely	About half the time	Most of the time	Very much so

I find myself getting in touch with my feelings.

1	2	3	4	5
Not at all	Rarely	About half the time	Most of the time	Very much so

I find I get feedback from other group members.

1	2	3	4	5
Not at all	Rarely	About half the time	Most of the time	Very much so

I find myself becoming more confident about being in a group.

1	2	3	4	5
Not at all	Rarely	About half the time	Most of the time	Very much so

Any additional comments: _____

_____

Forensic Psychiatry for Health Professionals. Chris Lloyd. Published in 1995 by Chapman & Hall, London. ISBN 0 412 48350 5

PROBLEMS ASSOCIATED WITH THE INSTITUTIONAL SETTING

A great many offenders have serious intrapersonal as well as interpersonal problems which have contributed to their unlawful behaviour. It is necessary for offender attitudes and behaviours to be modified so that their internal and external conflicts are resolved in constructive rather than antisocial ways. Therapeutic intervention should be promoted.

There are a number of conditions necessary for effective therapy, namely, a certain degree of trust – the client has to believe that the therapist is working in their best interest; confidentiality – clients need to know that the therapist will treat the material they disclose in groups with discretion; voluntarily engaging in therapy – the client needs to be motivated to seek help and desire change (Schlesinger, 1979).

This does not always occur and, where psychotherapy is practised in a prison setting, it is usually under less than desirable conditions. The prison environment is very different from the therapy setting in more treatment-oriented facilities. There is a high degree of surveillance; the therapist may have to wait on prison officers to escort the person, and, in some settings, prison officers remain present while therapy is taking place.

There are a number of barriers to providing effective therapy in the prison setting. These range from the physical surroundings, to the attitudes of inmates and staff. Forming a therapeutic alliance, the essential feature of psychotherapy, is very hard to establish in these settings.

In most prison settings, there is a lack of adequate space and furnishings, to provide an aesthetic environment within which to conduct therapy.

Offenders are more than likely prepared to view the therapist as a representative of the prison rather than being there to help them. Additional barriers include social class, ethnic identity and cultural variance which all greatly influence how one views and values therapy.

Staff attitude can play a key role in therapy not being effective. The attitude that nothing works does not provide any encouragement or support to either the inmate or the therapist (Mathias and Sindberg, 1985).

The prison subculture exists on the premise that exploitation of a person's weaknesses will take place. Inmates feel reluctant to let other inmates and staff know about their inner self as that increases their vulnerability. They feel most safe on a superficial level.

Confidentiality is difficult to maintain. Files are usually open to all staff members and there is little control as to how this information will be used. In addition, the inmate fears that any self-disclosed information will influence decisions about their case, parole eligibility, and so on.

Psychotherapy in prison facilities is often a planned part of the offender's programme of activities. The inmate may be reluctant to attend therapy and, once there, to become involved in therapy.

Kohutek (1983) further highlights that traditional psychotherapeutic techniques of group and individual psychotherapy have a number of disadvantages within a correctional setting. He defined these as being the small number of inmates that programmes actually reach, the stigma that is often attached to such programmes and the general lack of trust among inmate populations.

It is not only in prison that it is difficult to conduct psychotherapeutic programmes. Institutionalization manifests itself in a variety of ways: low self-esteem, fear of failure, repetitive and apparently meaningless behaviour, profound insecurity and difficulties in communication (Charlton, 1984).

Given that there are a number of different problems associated with running psychotherapeutic programmes in institutional settings such as prison and psychiatric facilities, more particularly the special hospitals, and maximum security units, the health professional has to carefully evaluate what type of programme to initiate.

SUMMARY

This chapter looks at the use of psychotherapy in an institutional setting. Particular emphasis was placed on the expressive arts therapies and how to go about establishing a programme using this media.

RESOURCES

Blatner, H. (1973) *Acting In: Practical Applications of Psychodrama Methods*, Springer Publishing Co., New York.

Gawain, S. (1978) *Creative Visualization*, Whatever Publishing, Inc. San Rafael, California.

Karasu, B. (1982) *Psychotherapy Research: Methodological and Efficacy Issues*, American Psychiatric Association, Washington.

Keys, M. (1983) *Inward Journey. Art as Therapy*, Open Court Publishing Company, La Salle, Illinois.

Naumburg, M. (1966) *Dynamically Oriented Art Therapy: Its Principles and Practice*, Grune and Stratton, New York.

Oster, G. and Gould, P. (1987) *Using Drawings in Assessment and Therapy. A Guide for Mental Health Professionals*, Brunner/Mazel Publishers, New York.

Pedder, J. and Brown, D. (1991) *Introduction to Psychotherapy*, 2nd edn, Tavistock/Routledge, London.

Rhyne, J. (1984) *The Gestalt Art Experience: Creative Process and Expressive Therapy*, Magnolia Street Publishers, Chicago, Illinois.

Smith, M., Glass, G. and Miller, T. (1980) *The Benefits of Psychotherapy*, John Hopkins University Press, Baltimore.

Yalom, I. (1985) *The Theory and Practice of Group Psychotherapy*, 3rd edn, Basic Books, New York.

REFERENCES

Birtchnell, J. (1984) Art therapy as a form of psychotherapy, in *Art as Therapy. An Introduction to the Use of Art as a Therapeutic Technique*, (ed. T. Dalley), Tavistock Publications, London, pp. 30–43.

Blatner, A. (1991) Theoretical principles underlying creative art therapies. *Arts in Psychotherapy*, **18**, 405–9.

Buxman, K. (1991) Humor in therapy for the mentally ill. *Journal of Psychosocial Nursing*, **29**, 15–8.

Carkhuff, R. and Berenson, B. (1977) *Beyond Counseling and Therapy*, 2nd edn, Holt, Rinehart and Winston, Inc., New York.

Charlton, S. (1984) Art therapy with long-stay residents of psychiatric hospitals, in *Art as Therapy. An Introduction to the Use of Art as a Therapeutic Technique*, (ed. T. Dalley), Tavistock Publications, London, pp. 173–90.

Feder, E. and Feder, B. (1981) *The Expressive Arts Therapies*, Prentice-Hall, Inc., Englewood Cliffs, N.J.

Goldberg, F., Coto-McKenna, S. and Cohn, L. (1991) Creative arts group process evaluation tool: Implications for clinical practice and training. *The Arts in Psychotherapy*, **18**, 411–7.

Golstein, S. (1990) You are what you read: The use of bibliotherapy to facilitate psychotherapy. *Journal of Psychosocial Nursing*, **28**, 7–10.

Greben, S. (1987) Psychotherapy today. *British Journal of Psychiatry*, **151**, 283–7.

Gunn, J. (1986) Education and forensic psychiatry. *Canadian Journal of Psychiatry*, **31**, 273–80.

Gunn, J. and Taylor, P. (1983) Rehabilitation of the mentally abnormal offender, in *Theory and Practice of Psychiatric Rehabilitation*, (eds F. Watts and D. Bennett), John Wiley and Sons, Chichester, pp. 115–28.

Hamer, B. (1991) Music therapy: Harmony for change. *Journal of Psychosocial Nursing*, **29**, 5–7.

Hobson, R. (1985) *Forms of Feeling: The Heart of Psychotherapy*, Tavistock Publications, London.

Kohut, H. (1984) *How Does Analysis Cure? Contributions to the Psychology of the Self*, (eds A. Goldberg and P. Stepansky), University of Chicago Press, Chicago.

Kohutek, K. (1983) Bibliotherapy within a correctional setting. *Journal of Clinical psychology*, **39**, 920–4.

Laing, J. (1984) Art therapy in prisons, in *Art as Therapy. An Introduction to the Use of Art as a Therapeutic Technique*, (ed. T. Dalley), Tavistock Publications, London, pp. 140–56.

Liebmann, M. (1984) Art games and group structures, in *Art as Therapy. An Introduction to the Use of Art as a Therapeutic Technique*, (ed. T. Dalley), Tavistock Publications, London, pp. 157–72.

Lloyd, C. (1987) The use of films and literature in the treatment of incest offenders. *Canadian Journal of Occupational Therapy*, **54**, 173–9.

Lloyd, C. (1987–88) The use of poetry in therapy: A case study of an incest offender. *Journal of the New Zealand Association of Occupational Therapists*, **38**, 7–9.

Lloyd, C. and Campbell, J. (1986–87) The therapeutic use of art in a forensic psychiatric setting. *Journal of the New Zealand Association of Occupational Therapists*, **37**, 10–3.

Lusebrink, V. (1989) In focus. Art therapy and imagery in verbal therapy: A comparison of therapeutic characteristics. *The American Journal of Art Therapy*, **28**, pp. 2–3.

Lusebrink, V. (1991) A systems oriented approach to the expressive therapies: The expressive therapies continuum. *The Arts in Psychotherapy*, **18**, 395–403.

Mango, C. and Richman, J. (1990) Humor and art therapy. *The American Journal of Art Therapy*, **28**, pp. 111–4.

Margo, G. and Manring, J. (1989) The current literature on inpatient psychotherapy. *Hospital and Community Psychiatry*, **40**, 909–15.

Mathias, R. and Sindberg, R. (1985) Psychotherapy in correctional settings. *International Journal of Offender Therapy and Comparative Criminology*, **29**, 265–75.

Melnick, M. (1984) Skills through drama: The use of professional theater techniques in the treatment and education of prison and ex-offender populations. *Journal of Group psychotherapy, Psychodrama and Sociometry*, **37**, 104–16.

Miller, I. (1989) The therapeutic empathic communication (TEC) process. *American Journal of Psychotherapy*, **43**, 531–45.

Pasquali, E. (1990) Learning to laugh: Humor as therapy. *Journal of Psychosocial Nursing*, **28**, 31–5.

Rogers, C. (1957) The necessary and sufficient conditions for therapeutic personality change. *Journal of Consulting Psychology*, **21**, 95–103.

Rosenberg, L. (1990) The use of therapeutic correspondence: Creative approaches in psychotherapy. *Journal of Psychosocial Nursing*, **28**, 29–33.

Schlesinger, S. (1979) Therapy on a treadmill: The role of the prison psychotherapist. *Professional Psychology*, **10**, 307–17.

Schramski, T. and Harvey, D. (1983) The impact of psychodrama and role playing in the correctional environment. *International Journal of Offender Therapy and Comparative Criminology*, **27**, 243–54.

Sheppard, J., Olson, A., Croke, J. *et al.* (1990) Improvisational drama groups in an inpatient setting. *Hospital and Community Psychiatry*, **41**, 1019–21.

Sluder, H. (1990) The write way: Using poetry for self-disclosure. *Journal of Psychosocial Nursing*, **28**, 26–8.

Truax, C. and Carkhuff, R. (1967) *Toward Effective Counseling and Psychotherapy*. Aldine Publishing Company, Chicago.

Walton, H. (ed.) (1971) *Small Group Psychotherapy*. Harmondsworth,
　　Middlesex, England.
Warren, B. (ed.) (1990) *Using the Creative Arts in Therapy*. Routledge,
　　London.

7

The use of activities

In designing programmes for forensic psychiatric clients, the use of activities is important in addressing issues relating to social interaction and basic activities of daily living. Activities can be incorporated into both the ward structure and in treatment programmes off the ward such as occupational, recreational and activities therapies.

This chapter aims to acquaint the health professional with the characteristics associated with activities and how they can be used in planning activity programmes. This chapter explores:

- context – environment
- social interaction
- planning the activity programme and
- example of an activity-based programme.

CONTEXT – ENVIRONMENT

The ward is the basic organizational unit within a forensic psychiatric facility. It is the place where the mentally abnormal offender will spend much of his time, perhaps years. If the ward is a maximum security ward, the mentally abnormal offender may not get to leave the ward to attend other programmes. Health professionals such as nurses who work in this setting may be rostered on for their shift and spend the entire day sharing the same physical space with people who may be violent and dangerous (Rossenrode and Cottingham, 1992). For this reason, it is important to consider ways in which to provide structure and planned activities on the ward to increase social interaction and participation for the clients and a more meaningful work environment for the staff. Major benefits include improved relationships and enhanced client coping (Radziewicz and Schneider, 1992).

Lyons and Menolotto (1989) suggest that activities in the form of interesting pastimes and productive tasks have a normalizing influence on a disturbed person's thoughts, emotions and behaviours, as well as promoting adaptive functioning in daily living skills.

The daily routine of washing, dressing, bed-making, eating, watching TV and so on all take place on the ward. The physical layout of the ward is important in the degree of ease clients are able to carry out these activities. It will also influence the types of activities that the staff are able to provide for the clients. The ward is very significant to both the clients and the staff; however, it is only one part of an institution and the service being provided. There are many organizational constraints which may hamper the actions that the ward staff might like to take, for example, planning a meal so that clients might participate in a cooking activity may necessitate filling in a requisition, having it approved, and then a number of weeks may pass before the food is available for the planned activity.

The activities used in forensic psychiatric facilities are greatly influenced by the total treatment context. Limitations on the kinds of activities which may be used are imposed by the environment, materials, equipment and available resources as well as the extent of the health professional's knowledge, skills, interests and ability. The health professional in a forensic setting will often be challenged to plan how to carry out activities in an environment which is not easily controllable but which is the reality for the clients living there.

When planning for an activity programme, it is necessary to take into account the realities of the staff and the clients who are likely to be involved. The teams within which health professionals work today are composed of a wider range of disciplines than in the past. It becomes a real challenge for health professionals to become more aware of the significance of personal biases and value systems as they will influence how treatment is thought about and carried out. There is a special need to be flexible and adaptable when working in secure environments. It is useful before instituting a new programme to involve the staff in some form of training so that they are familiar with the aims and objectives of the programme (Hall, 1983).

All wards have some type of atmosphere and there is the potential to create a more therapeutic environment. According to Barris and associates (1985), the task orientation of the ward is a modifiable factor that may play an important role in recidivism. They further state that programmes that are more successful in preparing clients to return to the community tend to have a high practical orientation which emphasizes organization and client involvement in tasks or activities. Programmes that have had a low success rate in keeping clients in the community tend to place little emphasis on planning client activities.

SOCIAL INTERACTION

The ability to communicate effectively with others is central to all forms of social activity (Willson, 1983). Difficulty in social interaction is a key issue that needs to be addressed when rehabilitating mentally abnormal offenders. According to Shepherd (1983), interpersonal relationships are essential for successful role performance and the ability to maintain social roles which are necessary in terms of social integration and adaptation. With illness or disability, the individual's ability to carry out required life roles becomes impaired. This then may relate to their usage of time, their habits, their skills, their motivation, and/or their beliefs and values. Reintegration into the community involves the individual in being able to carry out required tasks and roles within the family, in the workplace and in the community. The activity programme should be directed towards developing each forensic psychiatric client's functioning potential in order to achieve successful resocialization (Lloyd, 1987).

Persons with a psychiatric illness frequently have had chaotic, confused or destructive interpersonal relationships. In this specialized setting it is especially important to be aware of this and to pay attention to the interactions between the health professional and the mentally abnormal offender. It is the nature of the relationship which is a critical factor in achieving the desired processes of change (Lloyd and Maas, 1993).

Mentally abnormal offenders may have difficulty in developing healthy relationships with others which may at times make it difficult for the health professional to communicate empathy and respect. The mentally abnormal offender may have had previous negative experiences which results in loss of trust and feelings of insecurity. Distortion in perception may be evident, for example, there may be unrealistic expectation of the health professional. Other difficulties that may arise that influence the communication process between the health professional and the mentally abnormal offender include: pacing, restlessness, aggressive behaviour, hostility, abusive language, challenging authority, suspicion, irritability and indifference.

Clients need to know that they are cared for and valued as individuals in spite of their behaviour and past criminal involvement. Many offenders have extremely low self-esteem and can only begin to develop as they feel valued (Gunn and Taylor, 1983). Since health professionals are in a helping role they use their ability to help patients minimize problem areas and maximize their potential (Lloyd and Maas, 1991). It must be remembered that many of these mentally abnormal offenders will have difficulty in understanding their personal assets.

PLANNING THE ACTIVITY PROGRAMME

The clinical picture of mental illness is usually associated with an impaired pattern of social and daily life functioning. Clients often present complaints about a loss of interest in daily activities, that things that used to give them pleasure no longer do so. As a result of admission, the client's usual routines of self-care, work and leisure activities are further disrupted. There is a loss of former roles and associated with this, a loss of identity.

Activities may be utilized by health professionals to assist clients developing or maintaining skills required to successfully carry out their life task activities necessary for the satisfaction of personal needs and social roles.

If the activity programme is going to become a part of the ward programme the residents of the ward need to know what is going to happen. Clients should be made aware of the purpose of any activity so that they feel more able to accept and be a part of what is intended. One way of ensuring this is to have a house meeting, which could be held at the start of the week where all the patients and as many staff that are available could attend. At this meeting the clients should be encouraged to take some responsibility for themselves, for example, being chairperson, secretary, taking on ward chores and so on. The week's activities should be discussed and ideas and suggestions sought from the clients as to how they see some of their needs regarding the ward programme. A weekly schedule should be drawn up so that the clients are able to refer to the noticeboard or whiteboard to see what time certain activities are taking place.

Greenblatt (1988) suggests that it is important to have an understanding of interactive processes to help the health professional develop suitable goals and social skills for the clients. These include:

- intra-individual – there is no contact with another person or external object in the environment, for example, daydreaming.
- extra-individual – there is no contact with another person, the action is directed towards an object in the environment, for example, doing a crossword, latch-hook rug, jigsaw puzzle.
- aggregate – there is action towards an object in the environment while in the company of others but there is no necessity for interaction between participants, for example, bingo, movies.
- inter-individual – there is action of a competitive nature between two people, for example, backgammon, draughts, dominoes.
- unilateral – there is action among three or more people, one of whom is directing the action, for example, tai chi, an exercise group, aerobics.
- multilateral – there is action of a competitive nature between three or more persons, for example, card games, board games.
- intra-group – there is action of a co-operative nature by two or more persons intent upon reaching a mutual goal, for example, making a collage, painting a mural.

- inter-group – there is action of a competitive nature between two or more intra-groups, for example, volleyball, a sporting tournament.

The health professional requires an understanding of the level of social interaction necessary for successful participation in the activity programme. If certain clients are unable to relate to others on an individual basis it might be necessary to grade the activity so that there is progression from individual activity to that of being in a group setting. The meaning of an activity is unique to each person and is influenced by the individual's life experiences, life roles, interests, age, gender, cultural background and environmental context.

There are a number of aims that the health professional might wish to achieve by providing an activity programme. These may include:

- providing mentally stimulating recreation;
- promoting group harmony and mutual co-operation;
- promoting social interaction between members of the ward;
- encouraging increased levels of concentration;
- promoting routine and a sense of balance in daily life activities;
- maintaining existing skills and learning new skills, and
- promoting a sense of achievement and personal well-being.

Being able to successfully participate in an activity programme requires the individual to be able to function in the physical, cognitive and affective behavioural areas. Most activities will require that the individual have some degree of skills and abilities in each of the three areas (Greenblatt, 1988). If some impairment in levels of skills and abilities is evident it is important to focus on the existing abilities and potential of the individual.

A critical step in the development of a well-balanced programme is the selection of appropriate activities. There are a number of characteristics to consider when selecting activities.

- Activities should have some reason for their use.
- Activities should have some significance for the individual.
- Activities should involve active participation by the individual.

- Activities should enable the individual to feel a sense of achievement.
- Activities should relate to both the interests and needs of the client.
- The individual should have an understanding of the goal of an activity.
- Activities should be age appropriate and culturally acceptable.
- Activities should be able to be adapted if necessary.

There are a large number of factors to consider when selecting activities for use in the activity programme, including:

- selecting activities that will address the problems or needs of the clients;
- selecting activities that involve both psycho-social and physical elements;
- the property of the materials that will be used;
- the equipment or tools required;
- security limitations/safety precautions;
- preparation time required;
- complexity of the activity;
- how much direction is required;
- what type of learning is required;
- what type of communication is required;
- what level of decision-making is required;
- what the nature of the interaction is that is required;
- what level of attention span and concentration is necessary;
- selecting activities that the individual is able to achieve results;
- where will the activity be carried out;
- what level of staffing is required;
- what are the space requirements, and
- whether there is cost involved.

In activity analysis, each element of an activity can be broken down into individual components. By examining these components the health professional will have greater understanding of how the activity may help the client successfully participate. It allows the health professional to determine which skills and abilities are required by the clients.

Willson (1983) suggests that when breaking down an activity for activity analysis to look specifically at:

- the materials required,
- the tools required,
- the finished result, if any,
- the time requirement for the whole task,
- the environment which is most suitable,
- whether it is an activity for an individual or a group and
- the stages of completion (Willson, 1983, pp. 141–142).

In addition, Willson (1983) mentions a range of features for analyzing each part; these being:

- physical demands
- cognitive demands
- sensory or perceptual qualities
- social demands
- expressive opportunities
- independence
- practical considerations and
- the potential for grading (Willson, 1983, pp. 142–143).

Activity analysis further enables the health professional to modify or adapt selected activities which will allow individuals to participate. This is directed towards meeting the specific needs of the client population. It must be remembered, however, that too much change in an activity may lead to dissatisfaction being expressed by the individual. Therefore, it is important to adapt an activity only where it needs to be adapted.

Adaptation is a process that changes either an aspect of the activity or the environment to enable successful performance and to accomplish goals. Grading both individual and group structured activities may be required. The steps of an activity should proceed from simple to more complex. To start with, the activity should be presented at a level at which the client can succeed. The demands of the activity should increase as the performance skills of the client increase. The client should be encouraged to move away from inactive behaviour towards more interactive and productive behaviour.

Activity analysis and activity adaptation enable the health professional to plan for and select appropriate activities for such specialized client populations as mentally abnormal offenders. Activities are chosen to facilitate development or learning of skills and attitudes in the areas which will enable the client to function more effectively in work, leisure, self-care and social interaction.

An activity programme should encompass a wide range of activities to meet the diverse needs of the client population. Ideally, it should incorporate work, leisure and self-care elements to provide a balance in the individual's life as well as structure and routine. By including a variety of activities, the activity programme reinforces the value of a balanced routine or lifestyle. Activities may be classified in the following manner: social, diversional, work-type, intellectual, physical, creative and personal-care.

Social and diversional activities

Social activities provide the individual with the opportunity for fun and enjoyment. Some examples of social activities include: preparing and having afternoon tea, barbecues, an Easter egg hunt and celebrating special occasions. Diversional activities provide the individual with the opportunity for a sense of personal achievement. Craft work is an example of a diversional activity.

Work-type activities

Work-type activities provide the individual with the opportunity to have a balance in their lives. Some examples of work-type activities include putting away the linen, watering the garden, contract work and light industrial work.

Intellectual activities

Intellectual activities provide the individual with the opportunity for mental stimulation and continued awareness of the outside world. Some examples of intellectual activities include quizzes, current events group, a newspaper group and a discussion group.

Physical activities

Physical activities provide the individual with the opportunity for keeping fit. Some examples of physical activities include sport, exercise groups and aerobics.

Creative activities

Creative activities provide the individual with the opportunity for personal self-expression. Some examples of creative activities include drawing, painting, modelling, pottery, creative writing and music.

Personal-care activities

Personal care activities provide the individual with the opportunity to both maintain and improve upon various aspects of self-care. Self-care activities include grooming, hygiene and doing laundry.

The benefits of activities programmes

The selection of the activities used in the activity programme is made according to the functional or personal needs of the client. Activities form the link between a person's inner self and the external world. Results gained by the client through his involvement in activities include:

- learning about his abilities in relation to both objects and people;
- learning new skills and maintaining old skills;
- increasing confidence in abilities;
- physical needs can be fulfilled;
- having a channel for communication and self-expression;
- improving cognitive deficits, for example, in concentration span and memory;
- testing knowledge;
- maintaining links with the outside world;
- exploring and practising interpersonal relationships;
- taking care of personal needs, and
- developing competence and achieving mastery.

Through observation, the health professional gains information of the client's ability to self-organize, relate to other people and complete tasks. In addition, activities may be used as part of an initial assessment and as part of the ongoing evaluation process. This observation of the client's performance while involved in both structured and semi-activities, such as tending to self-care, provides useful information to aid in determining directions of treatment.

AN EXAMPLE OF AN ACTIVITY-BASED PROGRAMME

An example of a medium security forensic psychiatric facility and the programme they provide is illustrated below.

Elements of psychiatric dysfunction which occupational therapy addresses in treating forensic clients are cognitive organization, perceptual motor (visual, gross and fine motor elements) self-concept, object relationships, dyadic (paired) and group interaction, impulse control, frustration tolerance and reality testing. Individualized client treatment goals are established on the basis of data obtained about each client from interviews, functional skill assessment procedures and observations made during task performance within the occupational therapy setting. The occupational therapy programme provides the forensic client with an array of purposeful action-based activities which address themselves to the treatment goals.

Project groups afford client participants the opportunity to see cause-and-effect relationships between their behaviour and/or existing psychiatric problems and their impact on task accomplishment and interactions with others. The forensic client is provided the opportunity to observe and assess their own performance capabilities and receive essential feedback and/or direction from the therapists to enhance both treatment goal accomplishment and client skills development.

Individual goal objectives may include, but are not limited to the following.

1. The client will demonstrate improved cognitive organization in task performance.
2. The client will more realistically be able to recognize their own assets and limitations.

3. The client will actively explore various adaptive behavioural approaches with other clients.
4. Enhanced skill development will be demonstrated on self-chosen avocational pursuits.
5. The client will explore various action-oriented tasks to ensure more adequate need satisfaction in their current status, be it in-patient treatment, back in prison, or on the street.
6. The client will be more at ease, with reduced feelings of tension and anxiety due to legal predicament.
7. The client will interact in a more positive, co-operative and understandable manner when working in the presence of others or in a group situation.
8. The client will express both positive and negative feelings in a more socially acceptable manner.
9. The client will rechannel excessive aggressive energies into more appropriate outlets of expression.

Project groups occur on each of the three adult wards. Each ward meets twice a week for 90 minutes each session. Each ward group consists of no less that six and no more than twelve clients. Activities typically used include woodworking, leather work, ceramics and/or art media.

Clients must have been on the current ward for one week. Clients must be off 1:1 and/or dayhall restrictions and must be known to the therapist and not present any immediate danger to self or others. The charge aide or nurse should be consulted regarding questionable client behaviours.

Each client will be signed in and out from the ward book by the primary therapist assigned to that ward. Clients are then escorted to the occupational therapy area in the basement. Client requests for materials and tools are met and clients selecting new projects are guided and set up in their selection. Clients will work on individually selected projects sharing tools, materials and equipment.

When one occupational therapist is present for a group, a maximum of six clients are permitted to attend programming. When only two occupational therapists are present, a maximum of eight clients are permitted. No individual therapist is permitted to run a programme in the occupational therapy area unless a psychiatric security aide is present.

The primary therapist (the therapist assigned to a specific ward) will act as leader in the initial stages of setting clients up for a new activity. Co-therapists act as expeditors during each group, providing back-up in the ongoing carrying out of each client's activity. Directions and/or demonstrations of desired activity processes will be provided to clients as needed. Parallel group skills are a minimum requirement for participation in project groups.

The Admissions Ward Programme

The Admissions Ward Programme is held twice each week for approximately 90 minutes each session. Clients are encouraged to participate in the activities brought to the ward. The average number of clients for each session varies but is usually around eight. The programme facilitates improved interaction among clients and occupational therapy staff, while engaging in short-term tasks. It affords each client more constructive use of their time in a goal-directed manner. The programme provides a multi-purpose function for the therapist:

1. Staff get to know each newly admitted client and vice-versa.
2. It is possible to observe functional skill performance.
3. It provides an opportunity to observe behavioural responses.
4. It provides a system for data collection for purposes of initial assessment and reporting information at disposition staff conferences.

The Pre-Trial (Competency) Discussion Group

Pre-Trial (Competency) Discussion Group is held once a week for 60 minutes. Anywhere from six to ten clients participate. The group is designed for clients who are on a pre-trial status and who manifest confusion and a lack of understanding concerning their legal predicament. Clients are provided the opportunity to increase their awareness and understanding of current charges and of the various roles involved, i.e. the purpose of the judge, jury, district attorney and public defender. General procedures involved in courtroom situations are discussed through role-playing question-and-answer format and discussion of videotaped courtroom scenes.

The Cooking Group

There is a kitchen available in the occupational therapy area but due to limits in security coverage, it is not possible to add a cooking group over a lunch or dinner period. Clients, therefore, have been given the option of having snack groups twice a week. These cooking groups run during the project groups. Usually three to four clients out of the project groups choose to participate in the cooking groups. Upon completion of the cooking group activity, all clients share in the snacks. Cooking groups provide the opportunity to increase social interaction. The group is structured in such a way so that various roles can be assigned to clients to best meet their needs. Cooking also provides immediate gratification which appeals to a lot of clients.

The Project Group

Project groups are scheduled three times weekly for 90-minute treatment sessions. Generally, clients are allowed to choose when they want to attend, but there are always those who need strong encouragement to do so. Groups consist of eight to ten clients. The major activities utilized are woodworking, leather, ceramics and art work. Kits tend to be avoided, since many of these clients are more alert than the general psychiatric population; they are an active group which needs involved projects. Equipment which is used in the shop includes a jigsaw, radial arm saw, electric drills, sanders, assorted leatherworking, woodworking hand tools and kitchen utensils. All tools and potentially harmful materials are kept in locked cabinets and counted before, during and after groups.

The Juvenile Ward

The juvenile ward runs much the same type of groups as are on the adult wards. To be specific, there are two project groups a week and one cooking group. One major difference is that attendance is scheduled and required. The juvenile population differs from the adult in that generally their frustration tolerance is worse and they are less able to delay gratification. Consequently, kits and quick art projects are more frequently used. There is some limited amount of raw woodworking and leatherworking materials in the juvenile shop, but only a few juveniles progress to using these materials. Another difference in working with juveniles as opposed to adults is that the juveniles require more structure. For instance, in the juvenile cooking groups, all the supplies are pre-arranged and roles are assigned to the juveniles.

In order to continually meet the needs of the clients seen in this forensic setting, new groups are developed and seasonal groups are held. Some of the other groups that are held include community skills group, garden group, Spanish-English, English-Spanish groups, and various task format groups.

(This example is courtesy of Ms Karen McElroy, Norristown State Hospital, Pennsylvania, USA).

SUMMARY

The development of an activity programme is effective in providing the mentally abnormal offender with a sense of structure and routine. Additionally, it assists in restoring or maintaining the individual's abilities to function more competently in their daily life activities thereby developing appropriate social interaction patterns which are essential in being successful in the community.

REFERENCES

Barris, R., Kielhofner, G., Neville, A. *et al.* (1985) Psychosocial dysfunction, in *A Model of Human Occupation: Theory and Application*, (ed. G. Kielhofner), Williams and Wilkins, Baltimore, pp. 248–305.

Hall, J. (1983) Ward-based rehabilitation programmes, in *Theory and Practice of Psychiatric Rehabilitation*, (ed. F. Watts and D. Bennett), John Wiley and Sons, Chichester, pp. 131–50.

Greenblatt, F. (1988) *Therapeutic Recreation for Long-Term Care Facilities*, Human Sciences Press, Inc., New York.

Gunn, J. and Taylor, P. (1983) Rehabilitation of the mentally abnormal offender, in *Theory and Practice of Psychiatric Rehabilitation*, (eds F. Watts and D. Bennett), John Wiley and Sons, Chichester, pp. 115–28.

Lloyd, C. (1987) The role of occupational therapy in the treatment of the forensic psychiatric patient. *Australian Occupational Therapy Journal*, **34**, 20–5.

Lloyd, C. and Maas, F. (1991) The therapeutic relationship. *British Journal of Occupational Therapy*, **54**, 111–3.

Lloyd, C. and Maas, F. (1993) The helping relationship: The application of Carkhuff's model. *Canadian Journal of Occupational Therapy*, **60**, 83–9.

Lyons, M. and Menolotto, A. (1990) Use of magic in psychiatric occupational therapy: Rationale, results, and recommendations. *Australian Occupational Therapy Journal*, **37**, 79–83.

Radziewicz, R. and Schneider, S. (1992) Using diversional activity to enhance coping. *Cancer Nursing*, **15**, 293–8.

Rossenrode, P. and Cottingham , C. (1992) A New Zealand graduate certificate course in forensic psychiatry. Conference Proceedings, *Progress in Forensic Psychiatry*, Auckland.

Shepherd, G. (1983) Interpersonal relationships, in *Theory and Practice of Psychiatric Rehabilitation*, (eds. F. Watts and D. Bennett), John Wiley and Sons, Chichester, pp. 267–88.

Willson, M. (1983) *Occupational Therapy in Long-Term Psychiatry*, Churchill Livingstone, Edinburgh.

8

Vocational preparation

INTRODUCTION

The institutionalized person needs to develop basic task skills as a prerequisite for practical living skills. Being institutionalized, the individual may have lost whatever skills acquired in the past or may well have never learnt nor developed appropriate work skills. The forensic psychiatric person faces a dual stigma upon release/discharge when looking for and applying for work. Not only does he or she have problems concerning their psychiatric illness but they also have been labelled 'forensic' with all the connotations that that infers. It is necessary, therefore, that the health care professionals involved with this group of clients develop a programme that is comprehensive and covers such areas as career planing, basic job skills, graded work experience, interview situations and attitudes and feelings related to employment.

This chapter aims to acquaint the health care professional with the process involved when delivering a vocational preparation programme in a forensic psychiatric setting. This chapter explores:

- the importance of work,
- disability and work,
- limitations of the environment,
- the initial interview,
- vocational evaluation,
- treatment planning and
- examples of vocational programmes.

THE IMPORTANCE OF WORK

For the average person work is one of the most important social roles a person fulfils in a lifetime. It also takes up more time over a person's lifetime than any other single activity except for sleep. Work provides economic security, a sense of achievement, friendships and also helps to promote life satisfaction. A person tends to be identified by their work role since activities are associated with worth, value and legitimacy. Work and work-related activities, therefore, greatly affect a person's quality of life (Jacobs *et al.*, 1989; Kemp and Kleinplatz, 1985).

The degree to which work is valued as a worthwhile pursuit varies between socioeconomic and cultural groups. Culture plays an important part in how people view work. Individuals acquire behavioural patterns through belonging to a cultural group. This group influences the individual through a value system which is passed from parent to child (Holmes, 1988).

The type of work an individual is engaged in often defines socioeconomic status, lifestyle and quality of leisure time. Work and the associated benefits from having a job have an important impact on peoples' feelings of self-esteem and self-worth. Losing a job or not being able to find work can seriously affect the individual's well-being (Peterson, 1988).

DISABILITY AND WORK

The institutionalized person who needs to learn new work behaviours and skills may have never developed a work identity or role due to intermittent hospitalization or long-term institutionalization (Peterson, 1985).

People with psychosocial dysfunction often experience a variety of deficits that affect their chances of obtaining employment such as common negative symptoms, for example, flatness of affect and poverty of speech. In addition, they may display lack of intitiative, slowness and social withdrawal (Wing, 1970). It is these work habits, behaviours and interpersonal skills which often limit employability rather than actual task performance.

Inability to work or to be self-supporting often results in the person being stigmatized since work is a highly valued role that people are expected to carry out. Risch and Samuels (1971) consider that it is particularly difficult for the chronically mentally disabled to obtain work because of the reluctance of people to hire them.

Not only does work provide a sense of worth and value for the individual but it also provides a source of social contacts which help provide a normalizing social network which enables the person to make friends, to gain support, and to meet other people with whom they can share leisure pursuits. Work also provides the person with an income which helps them have a better standard of living and improved quality of life, and decreases their dependency on agencies designed to offer support for the mentally ill.

Jacobs *et al.* (1989) cite a number of studies that have shown mentally ill people, when vocational skills training and successful use of medication have enabled them to get a job and keep their job, have a low rate of relapse and readmission.

LIMITATIONS OF THE ENVIRONMENT

Fidler (1966) stated that a high percentage of people with chronic mental illness tend to return to hospital within a short time of leaving the institution regardless of the type of treatment received during hospitalization. It has been found that any behavioural changes which occur within the hospital are not carried over into the community setting. Later work by Hayes and Halford (1993) also discusses the difficulty with which clients are able to generalize the skills they learn in a treatment setting to outside that environment. This raises an important issue for health care workers in the field – how can programmes be designed differently so that clients are able to generalize adaptive behaviours to the community? It appears that programmes are not going to work effectively unless there is a combination of what the client learns in the treatment setting and exposure to the community environment that he is expected to function in, in the future.

The forensic psychiatric environment

The forensic psychiatric environment presents a unique combination of goals and limitations for vocational preparation.

Owing to the nature of the population, it is usually maximum security with many of the features of a prison. But it is also a hospital where the emphasis is on restoring mental health and instituting rehabilitation programmes designed to assist clients to function in a more socially acceptable fashion.

There are a number of limitations in designing and implementing a vocational preparation programme in a forensic psychiatric facility. Security is usually very tight and with this being the case many items made of materials such as glass, rope, metal, wood, etc. are usually considered to be contraband. If these items are allowed in work-oriented programmes it is usually under conditions of strict supervision. This then greatly restricts the type of work activities that can be carried out (Jacobs, 1991).

Client populations in these facilities may come from widely differing cultural, socioeconomic and educational backgrounds which also have an impact on how vocational programmes are designed. They may have come from impoverished backgrounds with no previous work experiences, or may have literacy and numeracy problems which means that a number of different treatment options may need to be considered before starting the vocational programme.

Clients in these types of facilities also face the dual stigma of mental illness and criminality; often the act that brought them into such an institution would have received wide coverage in the media, and they may well be discriminated against when trying to institute programmes that involve community experience.

An additional limiting factor is that of staffing and funding. It is not always easy to find the staff that wish to work in such an environment. And not all staff that do choose to work in forensic psychiatry choose to stay there for very long if they find that there are too many difficulties associated with the delivery of programmes. This then quite often leads to disruption of programmes that have been established. Funding is always an issue with much of the funding being allocated to security measures rather than creative treatment programmes.

The prison environment

Work-related programmes in prisons are diverse. There has always existed an ambiguity about prison environments. On the one hand, there is the idea of rehabilitation, on the other, there is the idea of protecting society from the offender and maintaining order within the institution. Prisons typically have a number of security levels which have a great impact on the different types of therapy and programmes that can be offered (Jacobs, 1991). The health care professional's role will vary depending on the type of facility.

Deming and Gulliver (1981–82) attribute the difficulty with therapy programmes in prisons to the fact that the public believes offenders should be punished and therefore, money is not put into treatment services. This then influences health care workers when making decisions about whether or not to work in the prison environment. The overall impact of this is that little is done to prepare offenders for re-entry into the community and for work.

A VOCATIONAL PREPARATION PROGRAMME

A vocational preparation programme consists of a number of steps to be followed including initial screening, initial interview, vocational evaluation and treatment planning.

Initial screening

Once the health care professional has received the referral for vocational preparation, the first step is to carry out an initial screening to determine the appropriateness of the referral. Ways in which to do this include:

- a review of records, for example, psychiatric, legal, social history and other related records;
- observation of the person's attitude, behaviour and interpersonal skills and
- an initial interview to obtain information relating to the person's work history and educational background.

The initial interview

The initial interview helps the health care professional to get to know the real person. It is important to create a non-threatening atmosphere and to encourage the idea of mutual co-operation. The initial interview is concluded with a mutually agreed upon assessment plan. The health care professional will be asking:

- Does the client have problems in the area of work-related skills?
- Will the client benefit from further evaluation?
- Is the client receptive to being involved in a vocational preparation programme?
- Does the client have a realistic idea as to their abilities, values and interest regarding employment?

During this initial phase the health care professional will be finding out about:

- Educational background – what year did the client finish school? were there any difficulties at school? did the client undertake any further studies of training?
- Employment background – what types of jobs has the client had? how long did they stay in a job? were there any difficulties at work? why did they leave their place of employment? were they interested in their job? what did they do well? do they have any references?
- Past experience in vocational rehabilitation – has the client been evaluated before? did they participate in a vocational rehabilitation programme? were they previously involved in work-release programmes, sheltered workshop or transitional employment programmes? did they previously have vocational counselling? what was their attitude/experience of vocational rehabilitation?
- Illness – how long has the client had a mental illness? has it interfered with working? have they had to leave a job because of illness? what sorts of difficulties does their illness pose for them?
- Legal – has the client a criminal record? have they committed an offence against their employer? have they ever been fired because of criminal behaviour? will they have to report to a parole officer?
- Support systems – does the client have family to provide support? do they have a network of friends? do they know where they will be going once discharged/released? do they know about follow-up?
- Social skills – how do they relate to others? what are their personal characteristics? are they able to be assertive? is anger a problem? are they able to cope with any stress?

The process of evaluation and vocational programming need to be tailored to meet the individual needs of the client. It is probable that clients will present for vocational preparation at differing stages in the course of their illness and length of time remaining for them in the facility. The health care professional must consider the client's ability to be evaluated, for example, literacy and the ability to follow written and verbal instructions are essential skills.

The initial interview will assist the health care professional in determining what type of evaluations should be used and the attitude and expectations of the client. One should observe for emotional reaction to be evaluated, for example, anxiety level, frustration tolerance, motivation and level of psychopathology. If the client is unable to respond appropriately, the therapist has the option to postpone completing the evaluation until the client is more settled or to modify the way in which information is to be gathered.

Case study

B. was an 18-year-old man diagnosed as having Klinefelter's syndrome. He was admitted for psychiatric assessment following charges relating to him having sexually assaulted his four-year-old niece. He had never held a job but liked the idea of being able to have a job. His main interests were horticulture and woodwork. He lives on a farm in fairly isolated conditions. The farm is no longer productive. His mother has arthritis and his father has a heart condition. B. spends a lot of his time involved in household duties. His brother, sister-in-law and niece live in another house on the farm. B. states he is very shy, and has difficulty in making conversation or in meeting people. He did not finish school, and had left two years previously. He had extra tuition in maths and English but was still not able to pass them. He was good at woodwork but always completed his projects far behind the other people in the class. At the current time he spends his time, when not doing household duties, working in his vegetable garden. He has a large vegetable garden and enjoys gardening. In addition, he does woodwork and makes toys. He goes out occasionally to play video games but does so on his own. He has thought about taking some courses but wasn't sure what type, and he expressed feelings of fear at the idea of taking a course since he wasn't sure how people would respond to him.

In looking at what B.'s assets and deficits were: He is socially isolated but has managed to be involved with a number of responsibilities and leisure pursuits. He expressed dissatisfaction with his current lifestyle but wasn't sure about how to institute changes. It was recommended that before undergoing further evaluation it would help B. if he attended a social skills training course as well as a literacy and numeracy course. This would increase his confidence level with meeting people, and provide him with some extra skills which he would require before undergoing further evaluation and any training courses.

Vocational evaluation

Vocational evaluation is a process designed to help people determine what kind of work they would like to do and what kind of work they are capable of doing. The identification and measurement of strengths are in terms of work skills, dexterities, aptitudes, rate of performance, vocational interests, work behaviours, attitudes and physical capabilities.

There are a variety of assessment tools and techniques that constitute vocational evaluation. The following work-related evaluation tools are available.

Psychometric testing

Psychometric testing involves basically paper-and-pencil activities. Interests, preferences, attitudes and values are determined. Surveys/inventories are designed to measure the client's interest patterns and vocational preferences. Aptitude tests measure the client's abilities in areas such as verbal, numerical, spatial visualization and perceptual speed; these tests will determine the client's strengths and weaknesses.

Behavioural and personality tests measure such areas as personality and intelligence.

Analysis of transferable skills

An in-depth review of the person's work experience is conducted and this is then compared to the requirements for specific jobs using a system of occupational classification using the Dictionary of Occupational Titles (DOT).

Work sample evaluation

Work samples simulate specific worker traits. Work sample evaluation is an approach which utilizes tasks, materials, tools and equipment that are similar to those used in an actual job. Work samples attempt to define skill, interest, physical capabilities, work behaviours and learning style. There are a number of commercially available evaluation systems, some of these being: McCarron-Dial Work Evaluation System, Philadelphia Jewish Employment and Vocational System, Singer Vocational Evaluation System, Talent Assessment Programs, Valpar Component Work Sample Series, and Wide Range Employment Sample Test.

Job tryout/situational assessment

The client is placed in a work situation, for example, an occupational therapy workshop, a sheltered workshop or an institutional work programme, for direct observation of client attitude, behaviour and skills. The focus is on how the individual adapts to the environment rather than on specific skills performance. The individual will work specific set hours, may receive an amount of money, will probably produce a product and must relate well with supervisors and co-workers.

At any point in the evaluation process, the health care professional may be asked to provide a recommendation for an individualized plan of action. Recommendations may include such things as:

- specific job placement
- work adjustment training

- job retention training
- behavioural skills development
- vocational training
- job finding training
- interpersonal skills counselling and
- literacy and numeracy courses.

Treatment planning

After the vocational evaluation process has been completed, the therapist writes a report based upon the data gathered during the assessment. The information may be presented in the following manner:

- demographic data
- presenting problem
- sources of information
- relevant work history
- testing completed
- summary of current status and
- recommendations for treatment planning.

The primary objective of the evaluation is to assist clients in achieving their vocational goals. Depending upon the identified needs of the client, a number of different types of treatment programmes and work experience may be organized. Some clients may need to work through a series of stages starting at the most basic level while others may be able to be slotted into the programme at a higher level.

EXAMPLES OF VOCATIONAL PROGRAMMES

Job Skills

Discuss past work experiences.
What do we gain from work?
What are our feelings relating to work?
What is entailed in a job, for example, hours, location, hazards, etc?
What makes a successful employee? Look at worker characteristics, work attitude, behaviour.

Discuss personal appearance and working.
How do you go about choosing a job?
How and where do you look for a job?
How do you go for an interview?
Provide information and preparation for those who have never held a job before and those who have previously been employed but tend to deal quite ineffectively with job stresses.

Career Planning

Look at employment interests.
What are your aptitudes and skills?
Discuss personality and working.
What is available in the community for gathering job or career information?
What sorts of courses/educational upgrading are available?
Investigate potential jobs.
How do you apply for a job?
Learn about coping with stress on the job.

Going for a Job

What are your vocational goals?
Learn to prepare a resume.
Prepare for an interview situation.
Role-play interview situations.
Discuss job stress.
How do you deal with job stress?
What are your personal assets/shortcomings?

Because clients have specific needs and will present at different stages, it is important to view the process of vocational preparation as a continuum of services.

In some cases the client may be able to progress through all the stages and in other cases as, for example, where the client is severely disturbed, they may be most secure and productive at an intermediate level such as in a sheltered workshop.

The idea of the continuum is that each stage is related to an overall goal of return to work to the degree that is appropriate for the particular client. If the difficulties of each stage are not satisfactorily coped with, the client's work capacity will be impaired to varying degrees. By breaking the goals into a series of steps it becomes possible to develop specific individual programmes for clients with thorough assessment and training programmes.

Vocational preparation of the forensic psychiatric client is a major focus of the total preparation for their resuming community life after hospitalization because there is an expectation that clients between 18–65 years of age may return to the workforce.

The vocational programme should be geared to promoting acceptable work skills in clients for whom work is a significant component of independent living. The programme offers opportunities for clients to assume progressive levels of responsibility and proficiency in preparation for work. Engagement in meaningful work activities promotes greater independence and normalization for the person returning to the community.

A whole range of other problems often impede successful work resettlement. Lack of motivation, decreased cognitive and intellectual ability, and the lack of self-confidence and social skills are the most frequently seen deficits.

All areas of functioning, that is, social skills, assertiveness training, and grooming and hygiene, need to be taken into account when considering vocational training. In addition, a number of other areas need to be considered for assessment and training if they have specific problems such as budgeting and the use of public transport.

AN EXAMPLE OF A VOCATIONAL PREPARATION PROGRAMME

Purpose:

To maximize the individual's potential for securing employment.

Objectives:

1. Provide information in order to increase the client's knowledge.
2. Assist the client to explore various employment-related topics.
3. Improve work-related skills and attitudes necessary for seeking and maintaining employment.
4. Lessen behaviours adversely affecting vocational potential.
5. Improve inter- and intra-personal skills.
6. Normalize and reinforce job-related skills and attitudes.

Components of the programme:

- basic job skills;
- career planning and
- going for a job.

Sheltered workshops/training areas

The client is monitored in a workshop setting with the objective of increasing satisfactory work behaviour. The client is expected to perform in workshop situations while learning specific manual skills, and encouraged to develop acceptable habits, tolerance and confidence at work. The ultimate goal for each client is to increase his work readiness and move him towards successful employment in the larger community.

Look at work adjustment behaviour:

- arriving at work on time
- attendance
- personal hygiene and grooming and
- work relationships.

Training programmes

Training programmes must meet the special needs of individual clients. Since it is unlikely that the institution can offer effective training programmes across many areas of client interest, it is often necessary to refer to other programmes.

Clients may go directly from training to competitive employment. Ongoing counselling/support services to help clients manage day-to-day problems are a useful way of insuring that clients are able to carry over the skills they have learnt in their vocational preparation programme; they require ample time to adjust to work experience outside of the institutional setting.

Adjustment to the worksite and change in lifestyle is often difficult, for example, locating transportation, managing a budget, integrating the demands of work and the demands of daily living, and finding a new place to live. These potential stressors may exacerbate symptoms, decrease stability and threaten the client's ability to hold the job.

Once clients have found a job it is important to maintain contact. It is essential to be aware of problems that clients may be encountering and help them to deal with these before they resign or get fired.

SUMMARY

This chapter has looked at issues surrounding the centrality of work for the individual and the implications this has for programming for clients. The important factors to be considered are accurate assessment and the design of vocational programmes that will meet the multifaceted problems of the forensic psychiatric client.

RESOURCES

Alberta Career Development aned Employment (1978) *A Job Seekers' Handbook*. Career Information Services. Edmonton, Alberta, Canada.

Anastasi, A. (1976) *Psychological testing*. Macmillan, New York.

Botterbusch, K. (1978) *Psychological Testing in Vocational Evaluation*. Stout Vocational Rehabilitation Institute, Menomonie, Wisconsin.

Buros, O. (ed.) (1938–1985) *Mental Measurement Yearbooks*. Gryphon Press, New Jersey.

Department of Employment, Education and Training. (1991) *Work Wise. A Self-Help Guide in Job Search* (4th edn). Australian Government Publishing Service, Canberra.

Grice, J. (1985) A practitioner's point of view: In search of the perfect evaluation. *Vocational Evaluation and Work Adjustment Bulletin*, 18, 4–7.

McCray, P. (1980) *Suggested Guidelines for Evaluation Work Samples*. Material Development Center, Menomonie, Wisconsin.

Pruitt, W. (1983) *Vocational (Work) Evaluation*. Walt Pruitt Association, Menomonie, Wisconsin.
U.S. Department of Labor (1977) *Dictionary of Occupational Titles*. Government Printing Office, Washington, D.C.
U.S. Department of Labor (1982) *A Guide to Job Analysis: A How-To Publication for Occupational Analysis*. Stout Vocational Rehabilitatoin Institute, Menomonie, Wisconsin.

Test instruments available from the following:

JEVS Vocational Research Institute, Philadelphia, Pennsylvania.
Singer Educational Division, Career Systems, Rochester, New York.
Tower, Rehabilitation and Research Center, New York.
Valpar, Valpar Corporation, Tucson, Arizona.

REFERENCES

Deming, A. and Gulliver, K. (1981–1982) Career planning in prison: Ex-inmates help inmates. *Vocational Guidance Quarterly*, **30**, 78–83.
Fidler, G. (1966) A second look at work as a primary force in rehabilitation and treatment. *American Journal of Occupational Therapy*, **20**, 72–4.
Hayes, R. and Halford, W. (1993) Generalization of occupational therapy effects in psychiatric rehabilitation. *American Journal of Occupational Therapy*, **47**, 161–7.
Holmes, D. (1985) The role of the occupational therapist-work evaluator. *American Journal of Occupational Therapy*, **39**, 308–13.
Jacobs, K. (1991) *Occupational Therapy. Work-Related Programs and Assessments*. (2nd edn) Little, Brown and Company, Boston.
Jacobs, P., Crichton, E. and Visotina, M. (1989) *Practical Approaches to Mental Health Care*. MacMillan, Melbourne.
Kemp, B. and Kleinplatz, F. (1985) Vocational rehabilitation of the older worker. *American Journal of Occupational Therapy*, **39**, 322–6.
Peterson, C. (1988) Pre-vocational assessment in mental health, in *Mental Health Assessment in Occupational Therapy* (ed. B. Hemphill), Slack, N.J.

9

Self-maintenance

INTRODUCTION

The institutional setting does not typically foster independence or feelings of worth in the individual. The individual is often apathetic and disinterested in taking care of personal needs. There is a sense of helplessness and powerlessness, a sense that there is litle point in trying to do things independently. Basic skills tend to be lost if the person does not make some attempt to take care of him or herself. Additionally, time often hangs heavily for the person. For the institutionalized individual time, and how to manage time, seems to lose its meaning.

This chapter aims to look at some of the ways the forensic psychiatric client can be assisted in maintaining a sense of worth and in taking care of basic daily needs. This chapter explores:

- self-esteem and thinking positively
- grooming and personal hygiene
- communication
- money management
- time management.

The general principles of running a self-maintenance programme for an offender population as compared with a non-offender population have much in common. The main difference centres around the fact that many of the forensic psychiatric clients will have spent years in closed and authoritarian institutions and will have developed secondary problems as a result of that experience. Typically, the types of clients requiring a self-maintenance programme will have a major mental illness such as schizophrenia, display chronicity with associated negative symptoms, show a marked loss of social functioning and have low self-esteem. Instituting a self-maintenance programme can assist these clients in maintaining their functioning at its present level and to avoid further deterioration.

A number of components make up the self-maintenance programme. Self-maintenance is basically practical and so the health professional should incorporate a large experiential component into the training. In addition, homework assignments are a useful learning tool to check whether the client is making progress with what they have been taught in the programme. Homework assignments emphasize areas that need extra work and give the individual direction.

The general aims of a self-maintenance programme include:

- assisting clients in gaining a better understanding of themselves and their behaviours;
- promoting development of new skills or re-learning skills that have been lost through institutionalization;
- encouraging exploration of alternative, more socially acceptable behaviours, and
- developing in individuals a positive view of themselves.

It is important that in organizing the programme, the health professional should:

- deal with immediate issues and concerns of the client;
- individualize the problem areas for the client;
- establish goals with the client that are concrete and have observable and measurable steps;
- build in ways of having ongoing monitoring of progress, and
- should provide for immediate feedback and positive reinforcement of any gains made.

After receiving the referral for the individual to be involved in the self-maintenance programme it is necessary to conduct an assessment. It is important not to underestimate the client's real level of functioning. Owing to how they feel about themselves, clients referred for this type of programme may well not let you know how they are really functioning. Talking through any of the assessments made should help the health professional clarify the situation.

SELF-ESTEEM AND THINKING POSITIVELY

According to Hopson and Scally (1980), people with a more positive self-concept are more likely to learn more, achieve more, care more, relate better and in general live more responsible, happy and fulfilled lives. The forensic psychiatric individual has usually had life experiences that have led to their receiving many negative messages about themselves and their behaviours. As a result, they often feel deeply inadequate, unliked, unwanted, unacceptable and unable. The tendency then is for the individual to put themselves down. Receiving further negative messages is like a confirmation of what the individual always thought, that is, that they are worthless.

Providing an environment where the emphasis is on recognizing and valuing the individual's positive qualities is necessary in having a basis for growth. Feeling good about oneself is related to a person's view of themselves and a feeling of something done well is a positive recognition of the person and their accomplishments, and aids in further personal development. Being positive about oneself is an important basis for learning, relating to others and being happy.

Self-esteem is made up of the thoughts and feelings a person has about themselves. These can be positive and/or negative. Self-esteem is greatly influenced by relationships with other people, for example, parents, teachers, employers and friends, and life experiences. How people feel about themselves – their self-esteem – can make a big difference in what they do and how they do it. Low self-esteem can create an unhappy life for the person who develops distorted perceptions of self and others. High self-esteem, on the other hand, helps the person to be who they want to be, therefore finding life more enjoyable and rewarding.

In developing a programme that centres around self-esteem and thinking positively, the health professional needs to encourage the client to:

- recognize that they and other members of the group are unique;

- recognize that they are valued and that being able to talk about oneself is important;
- learn to listen to others;
- relate to others' experiences;
- focus on the positive in self and in others;
- recognize what they as individuals have achieved, and
- establish goals for what they would like to achieve.

Some examples of groups include:

1. My good points

Hand out worksheets to the group members and have them fill them in. The types of things that could be asked are:

- what I like about myself
- what my good points are
- what I have achieved today
- what are my strengths
- I feel good about myself because ...
- what I like about another person in the group.

After they have filled in what the chosen area was for the day's session, they take it in turns to share this with other members of the group. The health professional should encourage the group members to relate to each other and to get people to identify what they have in common.

2. Self-esteem

In this group the health professional can either hand out worksheets for the group members to fill in and then discuss in the group or alternatively write the question on the whiteboard and encourage group members to come up with ideas and suggestions. Some examples of questions that could be looked at include:

- what is self-esteem?
- what things influence a person's self-esteem?
- what happens when a person has low self-esteem?

- how does a person feel when they have low self-esteem?
- what are some of the benefits from having high self-esteem?
- how does a person feel when they have high self-esteem?
- what can a person do to improve self-esteem?

Have each person identify one area that they are going to work on for the next session which can be then further looked at as the group sessions continue.

3. Self-confidence

Becoming more self-confident is one way of building self-esteem. The health professional highlights some areas that the group members could work on, for example:

- Being kind to oneself – look at the effects of labelling and discuss how what a person is, is not the same as what they do.
- Self-praise – have an activity in the group, for example, a collage, and encourage each group member to be able to acknowledge that 'I did that well'.
- Self-encouragement – look at what each group member would like to achieve and assist them in breaking this down into small easily obtainable steps.
- Being fair to oneself – have each individual group member write a list of the things they do well and share this with other members of the group.
- Being responsible for oneself – encourage group members to say 'I' instead of 'you' to take ownership of actions and feelings, highlight the difference between 'I think' and 'I feel'. Have the group members identify different feelings and what they feel about a variety of situations.

GROOMING AND PERSONAL HYGIENE

Grooming and personal hygiene are areas that the institutionalized individual frequently neglects. This is due in part to their feelings of low self-esteem and also to the extent or severity of their illness. Clients who are chronically mentally ill or who have been institutionalized for many years are easily identified by their appearance. It is typical to see poor physical posture, shuffling or slow gait, ill-fitting and poorly maintained clothing and unkempt hair.

Grooming and personal hygiene includes body, teeth, hair and clothing care. To determine the degree to which the individual is successful or independent in these areas a simple checklist will aid the health professional in deciding what the person's strengths and weaknesses are. This then will enable the health professional to structure the group according to the identifiable needs of the individual, and also for the appropriate level of instruction for training. Individual homework assignments can be incorporated into the programme so that group members have the opportunity to rehearse what they have learnt in group.

Group sessions in a grooming and personal hygiene programme need to have a practical basis with lots of hands-on experience for the individuals to assist in their gaining skills and confidence. The programme needs to incorporate demonstration, discussion, resource material and practice sessions. It needs to be at a pace that is comfortable for all the group members.

The health professional needs to aim towards assisting the client to:

- develop skills to carry out each task
- know when to carry the tasks out and
- know what materials or equipment are necessary.

Since the groups will be practical the health professional will be able to:

- gain information about the client through observing his participation in the tasks;
- monitor ongoing progress, and
- re-emphasize sections of the programme that the client might be experiencing difficulty with.

The overall aims for the client include:

- to learn new skills or rehearse existing skills;
- to improve the client's self concept, and
- to develop a sense of mastery in carrying out basic self-maintenance tasks.

Personal care group

Aim: To improve one's self-appearance.

Areas looked at:

- bathing
- teethcare
- haircare
- shaving
- nailcare

Media: Mirrors (both full-length and hand-held), brushes, combs, shavers (electric and manual), nail-file, nail-scissors, nail-clippers, deodorant, soap, handcream, toothbrush, toothpaste, makeup.

Structure of the group:

- Fill out the Grooming and Personal Hygiene Checklist.
- Each person tells the group what they have filled out.
- The health professional may direct the group for discussion by asking such questions as: 'What is the importance of good grooming?' 'How does it make you feel when you have taken care of your grooming and personal hygiene?'
- Review suggestions for good grooming.
- Points that the group members raise should then be written on the whiteboard.
- Show the group members the sample grooming tools.
- Demonstrate the use of the grooming tools.
- Have the group members practice using the sample grooming tools – initially this could be done by the therapist, for example, giving a facial, manicure, etc., then encourage group members to try for themselves.
- After using some of the sample tools the group should rejoin for further discussion about how it felt to have brushed hair, clipped nails or whatever specific task they worked on.
- Homework assignment should be given out based on what each individual would like to work on first.
- The group members are asked to keep a personal log about their appearance so that they are able to bring that back to the next group for discussion. This helps both the group

members and the health professionals to monitor progress made.

- Group members should be encouraged to keep a workbook in which all material about grooming and personal hygiene that is discussed in group can be written down, hand-outs by the health professional pasted in, and also the checklists and log that they keep. This provides the group members with resource material in addition to having an ongoing record of the changes they have been making.

GROOMING AND PERSONAL HYGIENE CHECKLIST

Name: _____

Date: _____

Please answer the following:

1. Bathing:

How often do you take a bath or shower? _____

Do you use a deodorant? _____

2. Haircare:

How often do you wash your hair? _____

How often do you comb your hair? _____

How often do you brush your hair? _____

How often do you have your hair cut or styled? _____

3. Shaving:

How often do you shave? _____

4. Nailcare:

How often do you cut your nails? _____

How often do you clean your nails? _____

5. Teethcare:

How often do you brush your teeth? _____

---

6. Appearance:

What do you like about your appearance? _____

What don't you like about your appearance? _____

What would you like to work on first about making changes to your appearance? _____

_____

Thank you for your co-operation.

Forensic Psychiatry for Health Professionals. Chris Lloyd. Published in 1995 by Chapman & Hall, London. ISBN 0 412 48350 5

MY PERSONAL CARE LOG

Name: _____

Date: _____

I am working on improving my personal appearance.

I will write down every time I do something about my personal appearance.

Personal Care	Mon	Tues	Wed	Thurs	Fri	Sat	Sun
Bathing							
Teethcare							
Haircare							
Shaving							
Nailcare							

What I am most pleased about

What I still want to work on

Forensic Psychiatry for Health Professionals. Chris Lloyd. Published in 1995 by Chapman & Hall, London. ISBN 0 412 48350 5

Clothing care group

Aim: To be able to take care of one's clothing.

Areas looked at:

- buying clothes
- washing clothes and
- mending clothes.

Media: A variety of clothes with manufacturers' labels on them indicating what type of material, and washing and drying instructions, soaps, detergents, ironing board, iron, and sewing materials such as cottons, needles, pins, buttons and scissors.

Structure of the Group:

- Group members should be encouraged to bring any of their clothes to the group that require washing and mending.
- Fill out the Clothing Care Checklist.
- Bring it back to the group and let the other group members know how the checklist was answered.
- Discussion centres around 'what is the importance of taking care of your clothes?'
- Ideas and suggestions should be noted down on the whiteboard.
- The discussion should then look at where the person can purchase clothing cheaply or obtain clothing, for example, looking at advertisements for sale items, alternative options such as St Vincent de Paul, the hospital itself, requests to relatives and friends.
- Look at how people tidy away their clothes – discuss why it is important to tidy away clothes. Then have people in the group either hang clothes up or fold clothes that require folding.
- Discuss how to wash and dry clothes. Have people in the group sort clothes (whites, coloureds, permanent press). Look at the labels the clothes have to find out washing instructions. Discuss temperature settings for wash and rinse and type and amount of soap/detergent to use.
- Demonstrate the use of the washer and drier. (Does it require coin change?)

- Have members of the group use the washer to wash their clothes; a drier may be used if available otherwise they may be able to hang their clothes out to dry.
- Discuss handwashing – delicates such as stockings, underwear – have members of the group do some handwashing.
- Discuss temperatures for ironing and look at the clothing labels for the temperature to iron (wool, silk, cotton, nylon). Have members of the group practice ironing.
- Demonstrate simple mending techniques, for example, threading a needle, knotting the thread, sewing on a button and mending a torn seam or dropped hem. Have the group members practice any clothing repair they might have that requires doing or alternatively have them practice on sample material pieces.
- Have a discussion about how they felt carrying out clothing care, any problems encountered, any further suggestions to make it easier.
- The health professional should provide handouts on the basic material that was presented in the group. This can then be pasted into their Clothing Care Workbook for resource material.
- Give homework assignments for all group members based on what they think they most need to work on.
- Ask the group members to keep a log of their clothing care and bring it back to the next group for discussion.

CLOTHING CARE CHECKLIST

Name: _____

Date: _____

Please answer yes or no to the following _____

Do you have any new clothes? _____

Do you know where to obtain clothes that you can afford? _____

Do you know how to sew on a button? _____

Do you know how to sew a hem? _____

Do you know how to sort clothes before washing? ____

Do you know what temperature to wash your clothes in? _____

Do you know what temperature to dry your clothes in? __

Do you iron your clothes? _____

Do you put your clothes away after wearing them? ____

Do you change your clothes if they are dirty?_____

Thank you for your co-operation.

Forensic Psychiatry for Health Professionals. Chris Lloyd. Published in 1995 by Chapman & Hall, London. ISBN 0 412 48350 5

MY PERSONAL LOG

Name: _____

Date: _____

I am working on taking better care of my clothes.

I will write down the ways in which I have done this during the week.

Clothing Care	Mon	Tues	Wed	Thurs	Fri	Sat	Sun
Change clothes							
Put away clothes							
Wash clothes							
Repair clothes							
Iron clothes							

What I am most pleased about

What I still want to work on

Forensic Psychiatry for Health Professionals. Chris Lloyd. Published in 1995 by Chapman & Hall, London. ISBN 0 412 48350 5

Since grooming and personal hygiene groups are time-consuming and lengthy, besides dealing with lower functioning clients, it is better if the health professional restricts group size to 4–6 clients, and to run the sessions several times a week. The group members need ample opportunity to practice what they have been learning and to receive positive reinforcement for any steps forward they make, no matter how small. It is usually a good idea to let ward staff know what the members of the group are working on so that they can encourage them to carry out the programme.

COMMUNICATION

Two key areas of communication that are important for the institutionalized person are that of basic conversational skills and maintaining communication with relatives and friends by letter-writing and the use of the telephone. Typically, institutionalized individuals feel isolated and powerless in their ability to communicate their needs to others.

In many facilities such basic things, for example, as wanting a cigarette, to use the telephone, write a letter all necessitate the individual to ask permission to do so. Life is very constrained with the individual being left with little freedom of choice. Nearly every aspect of life is governed by rules and regulations. It becomes important, therefore, that the individual learn how to frame requests and ask for help if required. If the person learns how to communicate basic needs in a more effective manner this decreases feelings of worthlessness.

People who are institutionalized frequently have difficulty in maintaining contact with family and friends. There is often little or decreased contact with the outside world. The individual's world, therefore, becomes very narrow with the loss of any roles and connection previously enjoyed.

The programme that is designed to assist the individual in communicating more effectively should focus on:

- face-to-face conversation
- conversation over the phone and
- written communication.

The health professional should use a 'Communication Skills Checklist' to determine the client's assets and deficits in communicating with staff and others. The one checklist can be used to gain an overall picture of the client's conversational and communication ability, although the actual programme would be best divided into three segments.

Conversation skills group

Aim: To improve basic conversational skills.

Areas to look at:

- initiating a conversation
- framing requests
- listening to another person
- being able to say no and
- responding to non-verbal cues.

Media: Worksheets, pens, role-playing, video-recording.

Structure of the Group:

- Have the group members fill in the Communication Skills Checklist.
- The group members then take it in turn to share what they have written with other group members. Other group members are encouraged to relate. Common themes are written down on the whiteboard.
- The health professional has a number of small cards on which are written various scenarios relating to conversational situations to use for role-playing purposes. These could include such instances as:
  - There is a new person on the ward and you would like to meet them.
  - You are on a long bus ride and would like to speak to the person sitting next to you.
  - You would like to ask one of the people on the ward to play cards with you.
  - You need to ask someone about finding directions.
  - You need to ask someone if you could use the telephone.
  - You would like to ask for weekend leave.
  - One of the members of the ward is always asking you

for cigarettes and you are getting tired of it.
- You want to relax and your friend is insisting that you go for a walk with them.
- You are waiting at the kiosk and other people keep getting served ahead of you.

- The group facilitator and co-facilitator select one of the cards to role-play the situation. The group members then have to comment on any observations about the interaction.
- The cards are handed around to the group members who have been divided into pairs. They are given some time to talk about how they are going to do the role-play before doing so. This is then videotaped with both of them having the opportunity to be the main person in the given situation. This is played back after each pair has their turn so that they can have immediate visual feedback as well as feedback from other members of the group.
- The use of video allows the people having done the role-playing to look at how they appear to others – points to look at here include: maintaining eye contact, showing interest in what the other person is saying, responding to both the content and the feeling of what is being said.
- Set the group members homework assignments and get them to fill in a Communications Skills Logsheet. This can be brought to the next group session for further discussion.

COMMUNICATIONS SKILLS CHECKLIST

Name: _____

Date: _____

Please answer the following

1. Do you feel comfortable meeting new people?_____

2. Do you feel comfortable starting a conversation? __

3. Do you feel comfortable ending a conversation? ____

4. Do you feel comfortable saying no?_____

5. Do you feel comfortable about standing up for yourself? _____

6. Do you feel comfortable asking for the return of something that has been borrowed? _____

7. Do you feel comfortable asking to borrow something? _____

8. Do you feel comfortable asking for help? _____

9. Do you feel comfortable using the telephone? _____

Forensic Psychiatry for Health Professionals. Chris Lloyd. Published in 1995 by Chapman & Hall, London. ISBN 0 412 48350 5

COMMUNICATION SKILLS LOGSHEET

Name: _____

Date: _____

Situation   Result

_____
_____
_____
_____
_____
_____
_____
_____
_____
_____

Forensic Psychiatry for Health Professionals. Chris Lloyd. Published in 1995 by Chapman & Hall, London. ISBN 0 412 48350 5

Depending on the stage of development of the group members, specific homework assignments can either be given or they can fill in their logsheets as situations arise.

Telephone group

Aim: To increase the person's familiarity with using the telephone.

Areas to look at:

- using a phonebook and
- making a telephone call.

Media: Phonebooks, pens, notepads, telephones.

Structure of the group:

- Discuss what it is about having to look up information and make phone-calls that make people feel uncomfortable.
- Look at the steps required to be effective when making or receiving a phone-call. List these on the whiteboard.
- Have group members practice looking up the phone-numbers of individuals and services that they require.
- Have group leaders role-play how to make a phone-call, carry on a conversation, receive a phone-call and take a message.
- Have group members break up into pairs and role-play making a phone-call, and receiving a phone-call.
- Have people in the group practice taking messages and reporting these back.
- Have group members identify who they would like to make a phone-call to, for example family or parole officer, and get them to try this out.

Written Activity Group

Aim: To maintain the person's links with people outside the institution.

Areas to look at:

- letter writing and
- special events.

Media: Paper, pens, pencils, paints, magazines, glue, scissors.

Structure of the group:

- Discuss feelings about family and friends and keeping in

touch with people. What does it mean to have those links with other people?

- Discuss the types of things that people can write in letters. Practice writing a letter.
- If any of the group members have no one specifically to write to, they might be encouraged to have a pen pal.
- At special times, for example Christmas, Easter, Mother's Day, birthdays, have group members make their own creative cards to send to family and friends.
- For those group members who may not have anyone they know outside the institution they can be encouraged to make cards for other people in the institution, volunteers, etc.

MONEY MANAGEMENT

For the forensic psychiatric client, skills in handling money may have deteriorated owing to their long incarceration, or managing money may well have been a significant problem area in the past. It is an important skill for successful independent functioning.

Kaseman (1981) identified that poor money management skills were a common problem for discharged psychiatric clients, and that they frequently believed that their best option was to return to the protection of the hospital.

The health professional should design a programme that looks at a wide range of issues – from money identification to banking and budgeting. The money management group should have a practical orientation with group members having ample opportunity to become familiar with both handling money and how to manage their money.

Money management group

Aim: To increase the individual's ability to handle money successfully.

Areas to look at:

- money recognition
- having an account – withdrawals, deposits and
- budget.

Media: Coins, notes (genuine currency), play money, withdrawal and deposit slips, pencils, items to buy – for example, combs, toothbrushes, paperbacks, etc. – price tags, workbooks.

Structure of the group:

- Administer the Money Management Checklist.
- Have group members share what they have written with other group members. Discussion centres around some of the problems that members of the group have in common.
- Introduce the group members to the types of coins and notes that are in current usage, and explain the units of money.
- Give each member of the group a certain amount to spend and an item they wish to buy. Get them to work out how much change they should receive.
- Give each member of the group a list of basic items and the amounts they cost and have them make a tally.
- Have the group members divide up into pairs so that one person can role-play the consumer and the other the cashier. Have them practice buying various items and in receiving change. They can then reverse roles.
- Have a general discussion about buying items, handling money and receiving change. Are there any problems or difficulties?
- Show group members what deposit and withdrawal forms are. Demonstrate filling them in. Have all group members practice filling them in.
- Discuss what a bank and other financial institutions are and what they do for people. Why is it important to be able to make use of them? If group members are allowed to leave the institution take them on a field trip to visit some near-by financial institutions.
- Discuss why having a budget helps in money management. Write down ideas people come up with on the white-board.
- Issue worksheets and have group members try to identify how they spend their money. Bring this back to the group for general discussion. This promotes an awareness of spending habits.

- Look at the importance of being able to establish short- and long-term goals. Issue a worksheet and have group members try to identify some short- and long-term goals for themselves.
- Discuss the concept of fixed and flexible expenses. Issue a worksheet to group members and help them fill it out. Bring back to the group for further discussion.
- Have each group member make up a sample of a weekly budget of spending money only, for example, cigarettes, soap, drinks etc.
- Have homework assignments such as keeping a record of how much spending money was spent during the week. Bring this back to the group for discussion – were people able to live with what they had to spend or did they need to borrow?

MONEY MANAGEMENT CHECKLIST

Name: _____

Date: _____

Please answer the following

1. Do you have difficulty recognizing the various units of money? _____

2. Do you have difficulty in counting your change to see if it is correct? _____

3. Do you have difficulty in filling in a withdrawal form? _____

4. Do you have difficulty filling in a deposit form? ____

5. Do you have difficulty in saving money? _____

6. Do you have difficulty in working out a budget? ____

7. Do you have difficulty in keeping track of how you spend your money? _____

8. Do you have difficulty in setting money management goals? _____

9. Do you have difficulty in identifying fixed and flexible expenses? _____
10. Would you like to change how you manage your money? If so, in what way?_____

Forensic Psychiatry for Health Professionals. Chris Lloyd. Published in 1995 by Chapman & Hall, London. ISBN 0 412 48350 5

TIME MANAGEMENT

The forensic psychiatric individual is likely to experience a wide range of problems. They often have difficulty in organizing, poor judgement in the management of personal life, a lack of balance in daily routines and a poor sense of time.

In designing a time management programme the health professional needs to:

- determine the way in which the individual spends time;
- promote awareness in the individual about their usage of time, and
- identify the ways the individual would like to spend their time.

Time management group

Aim: To make better personal use of time.

Areas to look at:

- how the individual spends their time;
- how the individual thinks and feels about their use of time;
- identifying priorities in the way the individual uses their time, and
- identifying the things the individual would like to do.

Media: Worksheets, pens.

Structure of the group:

- Have the members of the group fill out the two parts of the form 'How I Spend My Week'.
- Have each group member share with others in the group

about how they spend their time. Encourage relating and highlight things group members may have in common.

- Next have each person identify whether the activity was something they wanted to do or had to do.
- Centre discussion around 'How do we feel when we have to do things?' 'Are we interested in doing them?' 'Do we do them well?' 'Can we approach things differently?'
- Have group members write down how many hours they spend in a day doing certain activities. Have a discussion on this: 'Is my day balanced?' 'Is there a different way to do things?'
- Discuss the need to organize one's time to make time spent on various activities more rewarding. Have an assignment on 'What my priorities are'.
- Discuss the things a person would like to do. Have group members fill out the 'I would like to do' form. Look at what is realistic and practical – Do you want to do it alone or with others? Is it a familiar activity or something new?
- Introduce the idea of trying something different in each individual's daily routine, for example, taking up a hobby, playing cards, etc. Have each group member decide what they will try out during the week and ask them to report back in the next session.

HOW I SPEND MY WEEK (Part 1)

Name: _____

Date: _____

Morning	Mon	Tues	Wed	Thurs	Fri	Sat	Sun
7–7.30							
7.30–8.00							
8–8.30							
8.30–9.00							
9–9.30							
9.30–10.00							

10–10.30
10.30–11.00
11–11.30
11.30–12.00
Afternoon
12–12.30
12.30–1.00
1–1.30
1.30–2.00
2–2.30
2.30–3.00
3–3.30
3.30–4.00
4–4.30
4.30–5.00
5–5.30
5.30–6.00
Evening
6–6.30
6.30–7.00
7–7.30
7.30–8.00
8–8.30
8.30–9.00
9–9.30
9.30–10.00
10–10.30
10.30–11
11–11.30
11.30–12.00

Forensic Psychiatry for Health Professionals. Chris Lloyd. Published in 1995 by Chapman & Hall, London. ISBN 0 412 48350 5

HOW I SPEND MY WEEK (Part 2)

Name: _____

Date: _____

List: 'What I had to do'   Number of hours

_____

_____

_____

_____

_____

_____

_____

List: 'What I wanted to do'   Number of hours

_____

_____

_____

_____

_____

_____

Forensic Psychiatry for Health Professionals. Chris Lloyd. Published in 1995 by Chapman & Hall, London. ISBN 0 412 48350 5

WHAT MY PRIORITIES ARE

Name: _____

Date: _____

List the things that are important for you to do this week.

Mon   Tues   Wed   Thurs   Fri   Sat   Sun

Forensic Psychiatry for Health Professionals. Chris Lloyd. Published in 1995 by Chapman & Hall, London. ISBN 0 412 48350 5

I WOULD LIKE TO DO

Name:_____

Date: _____

List 6 things I'd like to do	Alone or with others	New or old

What I would like to do best _____

My target date for trying what I would like to do best
_____

How successful have I been? _____

Forensic Psychiatry for Health Professionals. Chris Lloyd. Published in 1995 by Chapman & Hall, London. ISBN 0 412 48350 5

SUMMARY

This chapter has looked at ways in which a self-maintenance programme can be established. The components of the programme should be integrated with having as the overall goal an increased sense of worth and ability to manage the self in basic self-maintenance tasks.

RESOURCES

Alberta Consumer and Corporate Affairs. (1985). *Taking charge of your money*. Alberta Consumer and Corporate Affairs, Edmonton.

Hughes, P. and Mullins, L. (1981). *Acute psychiatric care. An occupational therapy guide to exercises in daily living skills*. Charles B. Slack, Inc, Thorofare, N.J.

Kartin, N. and Van Schroeder, C. (1982). *Adult Psychiatric Life Skills Manual*. Schroeder Publishing and Consulting, Kailu, Hawaii.

REFERENCES

Hopson, B. and Scally, M. (1980). *Life skills teaching programmes*, Lifeskills Associates, Leeds.

Kaseman, B. (1981). Teaching money management skills to psychiatric outpatients. *Occupational Therapy in Mental Health*, **1**, 59–71.

10

Social interaction

INTRODUCTION

Effective inter- and intrapersonal skills are required to survive in environments such as prison and forensic psychiatric facilities, as well as the environment outside the institution. The individual needs to be alert to the environment and the way in which he or she comes across to others. Dysfunction may be evident in self-concept, interpersonal relationships, impulse control, frustration tolerance and lack of responsibility for actions. Therapeutic intervention is directed towards developing in the individual a greater awareness of self and of others.

This chapter aims to look at a number of ways that the individual can be assisted to develop a more effective style of social interaction. This chapter explores:

- relationship-making skills
- assertiveness and
- anger management.

SOCIAL ACCEPTANCE

According to Folts (1988), the ability to interact effectively with others in a social community environment has been ascribed by society as a critical factor for peer acceptance. It is central to a person's adjustment in life and in being happy and satisfied with life experiences. People interact with other people on all sorts of different occasions and levels: shops, transport, accommodation, work, friends, family and so on. Life, and the meaning or quality of it, depend very much on a person being able to share ideas, give opinions, seek information, explain needs, express feelings and feel confident in doing so.

Who would benefit?

Some people may never have acquired the skills necessary for meaningful social relationships. This may have been the result of such factors as poor parental modelling, restrictive environments, lack of opportunity, and the attitudes and beliefs the person holds about themselves.

Additionally, poor social functioning can also exist as a result of mental illness. The ability to engage in appropriate social behaviour may have been temporarily disrupted by the illness or may well have been a longstanding associated problem.

For those people who have had a long stay in an institution such as a psychiatric hospital or a prison, a different form of social behaviour develops. These types of institutions have a well-defined subculture with its own mores and norms which is unique and not related to the social community outside the institution.

Poor social functioning makes it difficult for the institutionalized person to communicate or relate to the wider community. This, therefore, puts them at a distinct disadvantage in becoming accepted and being integrated into the community. This in turn leads to further isolation, loneliness, rejection and low self-worth (Drew, 1991).

In looking at a person's level of social functioning the extent and nature of it may vary. For example, it may involve a specific behaviour such as eye-contact or may relate to a particular situation, such as talking to the opposite sex. Looking at social functioning may involve a more global picture, for instance when looking at chronic mentally ill people who have been institutionalized for many years and have become non-interactive and socially isolated.

ASSESSMENT

Before deciding upon which type of therapy would be most beneficial in assisting the person's social readjustment and subsequent return to the community, it is necessary to conduct an assessment. The assessment will highlight the person's assets and deficits and provide direction for treatment. The assessment could include a combination of:

- discussion with various staff members who interact with the person at different times and for different reasons;
- observation of the person in the ward or programme environment;
- an initial interview to gather information about how the person views their interpersonal and social relationships;
- checklists or rating scales that specify what behaviours are being observed, and
- self-reporting by clients on their social behaviour.

Ongoing assessment is an important feature in a training programme that focuses on social behaviour. Programmes should always be designed with the particular needs of the client(s) in mind. Ongoing assessment is useful in that the progress of the client is monitored, and the effectiveness of the programme is evaluated. Modifications may have to be made to the programme if the required changes are not being achieved.

An example of a checklist to observe a person's social behaviour:

SOCIAL INTERACTION OBSERVATION SCALE

Name: _____

Date: _____

Please rate the following:

	Inappropriate				Appropriate
	1	2	3	4	5
Eye contact					
Facial expression					
Posture					
Clarity of speech					
Content of speech					

	1	2	3	4	5
Initiates conversation					
Maintain conversation					
Makes requests					
Asks for information					
Listens to others					
Seeks others out					

Forensic Psychiatry for Health Professionals. Chris Lloyd. Published in 1995 by Chapman & Hall, London. ISBN 0 412 48350 5

TREATMENT PLANNING

There are a number of steps to follow before starting the treatment programme:

- review assessment data
- identify problem
- explain the programme and
- set goals.

The health professional needs to have a clear understanding of the assets and deficits of the person referred to the programme. Specific relationships and situations should have been looked at. In addition, the person should be encouraged to identify where he or she is doing well.

Clients themselves should acknowledge that they have a problem in the area of social behaviour. If they do not accept that they have a problem it is unlikely that they will be motivated to actively participate in the programme. They must view making changes about a particular problem as being necessary to their needs.

The health professional needs to determine whether or not a social behaviour training programme is appropriate for the client. It may be that some other form of treatment would be more appropriate, for example, individual cognitive behavioural strategies.

The client needs to agree to participate in the training programme. The health professional will need to explain the nature of the programme, when the programme will be run, for how long, how often, location, who will be involved, and that it involves active participation and that homework assignments will be given.

Goal setting should be a collaborative effort between the health professional and the client. The goals should be realistic and related to the person's everyday life. They should be graded according to skill deficiency into small steps, specific, and behavioural. The more simple goals should be tackled first before moving on to harder, more complex, goals.

TREATMENT IMPLEMENTATION

The health professional makes a decision as to whether to use individualized or standardized training programmes. There are a number of programmes that are readily available either utilizing video or providing structured written exercises to follow. Or, depending on the identifiable needs of the clients and the type of facility and availability of resources, the health professional might elect to design a programme. Before initiating the programme, it is necessary to provide an outline specifying:

- title of the programme;
- contact person;
- objectives of the programme;
- investigation of needs for programme;
- group composition;
- means of gaining access to the programme;
- location;
- time, frequency, and length of sessions;
- number of staff involved;
- outline of each session, including homework assignments and use of media, and
- proposed evaluation of the programme.

To ensure the effectiveness of the programme, it is a good idea to notify staff about who will be in the programme and request their assistance in helping clients practice the skills they are learning outside the group sessions.

THE USE OF BEHAVIOURAL ASSIGNMENTS

Many programmes might be effectively designed, and yet the health professional may be frustrated by the seeming lack of success of the programme. An important issue that needs to be considered is that of the transfer of skills outside of the therapy sessions. One way of increasing the likelihood of transfer of skills is that of prescribing activities and homework assignments, to enable the client to rehearse what has been learnt in therapy.

Homework assignments, according to Shelton and Levy (1981), can have a number of useful benefits:

- Therapy is able to continue without the presence of the health professional.
- New behavioural patterns are able to be practised and tried out in different settings and situations.
- The client has a sense of increased self-control.
- Transfer of treatment adds to the client's social environment.
- Clients involved in their own treatment planning are more likely to maintain therapy gains over time.

Case studies of clients with deficits in appropriate social behaviour:

---

1. Bill is 49 years old with a diagnosis of chronic schizophrenia. He has been institutionalized for the last 20 years. The treatment team have determined that he should be prepared to live in supportive accommodation outside the hospital setting. He paces around the ward, talks incessantly, interrupts other people when they are talking and doesn't always listen to what is being said. He does not like to sit close to people and when in a group prefers to stay outside the group. He has problems relating to women, saying he doesn't like them.

---

2. Steve is a 19-year-old youth. He stabbed a policeman while he was thought to have paranoid delusions. The diagnosis is still being determined and he is in hospital for

ongoing assessment. He spends all of his available spare time sleeping on a couch in the ward loungeroom. When he is involved in groups or assigned activities he sits very still with head bent and eyes lowered. He does not approach anyone or initiate conversation. He will respond appropriately when spoken to directly but in a monosyllabic manner without looking at the person.

3. John is a 32-year-old man with a diagnosis of personality disorder and has a long history of anti-social acting-out behaviour mostly directed towards his mother. He was hospitalized following an incident where he stabbed his mother. On the ward he sits in an out-of-the-way place and does not approach anyone. He will answer staff if spoken to directly but ignores other people. He has difficulty in both initiating and maintaining conversation.

4. Mary is 29 years old and is mentally handicapped. When she doesn't understand what is happening or thinks that people are talking about her, she screams at the person and either hits or kicks them. Although she has had few problems relating to staff on the ward or older people, she has difficulty relating to the younger people on the ward, particularly young males.

5. Pat is 35 years old with a diagnosis of personality disorder, psychopathic type. He is in hospital as a result of assaulting a person he didn't know. He appears surly and bad-tempered, and spends most of his time glowering at people. He has had long-standing difficulties in getting along with people, is easily roused to anger and responds by punching the person.

6. Dave is 63 years old with persistent delusions concerning fire. He was hospitalized after he committed a series of acts of arson. On the ward he appears to be pleasant and polite, although he tends to keep to himself and will not initiate any activities that involve other people.

THE SOCIAL INTERACTION PROGRAMME

Rationale for the social interaction programme

In this programme, consisting of three main components, there is a focus on the following:

- relationship-making skills, since many institutionalized individuals, and in particular, the chronically mentally ill, have deficits in the most basic communication skills;
- assertiveness training, since many institutionalized individuals feel powerless and unable to make any impact on their immediate social enviornment, and
- anger management, since a large percentage of institutionalized individuals, especially those in the special hospitals, have shown poor impulse control, and violent, aggressive behaviour.

Relationship-making skills

Aim: To increase awareness of the basic communication skills required to form relationships with other people, that is, sending and receiving messages both verbally and non-verbally.

Media: paper, pens, magazines, glue, scissors, role-play, discussion, whiteboard.

Structure of the group:

1. Introduction/warm-up – The health professional introduces the purpose of the group and the topic that they will be working on for that session. The warm-up involves the group members introducing themselves and saying something

about themselves that they'd like other people to know. After the initial group, the beginning of the group should look at how group members have carried out their homework assignments.

2. Discussion/activity – The next section of the group involves carrying out an activity and having a disussion about it. The health professional might utilize a number of different ideas and techniques to engage the group members.

Examples include:

- Write the word 'communication' on the board and ask group members for any ideas they might have about what it means. Discuss the basic elements of communication. Ask each group member who they have talked to the previous day, what was it about and how they felt about this.
- Discuss non-verbal communication and how facial expressions and body posture indicate people's feelings. Show group some pictures of different examples to demonstrate. Hand out drawings to group members of a face that is either happy or sad and have people write down how the person might be feeling and possible reasons for it. Then bring it back to the group for further discussion on non-verbal communication.
- Have group members look through magazines to find pictures of people with a range of different expressions. Have them develop a theme and make the cut-out into a collage. Bring back to the group for discussion.
- Have group members break up into pairs and get them to draw each other using large sheets of paper so that the person can be drawn to life-size. Ask them to write down a list of things/qualities they notice about the other person. Bring it back to the group for discussion about what they see in the other person.
- Have each member of the group say what they like about another member of the group. Then have group members identify what it is about a person that makes them likeable – list these good points on the board. Finish up by having each person say one good thing about themselves.
- Have people break up into pairs and have a short conversation – getting to know the other person. They then bring

this back to the group to introduce who they were talking to and what they found out about the other person.

- Select some specific examples of social interaction for each group member to role-play. It should be related to their current situation – starting a conversation, making a request, asking for information. The group leader and co-leader should role-play the scenario first, then have the group members do so. This should be videotaped and played back after each person has their turn for immediate feedback (both from seeing themselves and from hearing from other group members).

3. Homework assignments should be given out at the end of the session for group members to work on when not in group. The health professional should start with small homework assignments and gradually increase assignments. This should then be brought back to the following group session for discussion. Examples of homework assignments:

- Smile at two people.
- Ask someone to play cards.
- Ask someone how they are feeling.
- Tell someone what you like doing.
- Give someone a compliment.

To keep track of how their homework assignments are going it is best to have the group members keep a log that they can fill in and bring to group. For example:

MY COMMUNICATION LOG

Name:

Who I talked to	For what reason	With what result

Forensic Psychiatry for Health Professionals. Chris Lloyd. Published in 1995 by Chapman & Hall, London. ISBN 0 412 48350 5

MY COMMUNICATION GOALS

Name: _____

I will say good morning to two people in the morning.

Who _____

When _____

Result _____

I will ask another patient to sit with me at the dinner table.

Who _____

When _____

Result _____

I will have a conversation with at least two people during the day.

Who _____

When _____

Result _____

I will make a request for information.

Who _____

When _____

Result _____

Forensic Psychiatry for Health Professionals. Chris Lloyd. Published in 1995 by Chapman & Hall, London. ISBN 0 412 48350 5

4. Wrap-up – The wrap-up concludes the session. It should be short and briefly summarize the topic that was worked on in the day's session. Group members should be asked if they have any questions or comments to make.

Assertiveness training

Aim: To enable people to become more comfortable about being assertive.

Media: situations written on index cards, paper, pens, whiteboard, role-plays, discussion.

Structure of the group:

1. Introduction/warm-up – The group leader introduces the topic of assertiveness, briefly outlining the benefits from assertive behaviour, and how it contrasts with aggression or non-assertiveness and what these communicate to another person. In the warm-up, each person introduces themselves and say what they hope to achieve by being in the group.

2. Discussion/activity – Each session will consist of an activity which involves responding to situations requiring assertiveness. After the initial session, people will report back to the group the results of their homework assignment. This will be followed by feedback and general discussion exploring assertion and how people feel about what they have been doing. There are a number of activities that the therapist can utilize to demonstrate assertiveness, for example:

- distribute an Assertiveness Checklist to each patient and ask them to fill it in. This can then be shared with other members of the group, with the group leader encouraging various group members to relate what they have in common about how they handle the different situations listed.

ASSERTIVENESS CHECKLIST

Name: _____

Date: _____

Please answer the following:

I find it difficult to say no when someone asks to borrow something _____

I find it difficult to say no when I am asked to do something I don't wish to do _____

I find it difficult to stand up for myself _____

I find it difficult to accept a compliment _____

I find it difficult to say something nice to another person

_____

I find it difficult to return items I have purchased to the shop _____

I find it difficult to talk about my feelings _____
I find it difficult to start a conversation with strangers
_____

I find it difficult to do something new or different
_____

I find it difficult to ask for help _____

Forensic Psychiatry for Health Professionals. Chris Lloyd. Published in 1995 by Chapman & Hall, London. ISBN 0 412 48350 5

*Use situation and response cards which have a number of everyday interactions listed with an example of assertive, non-assertive, and aggressive responses, for example:

Situation: You are watching your favourite TV show and someone walks into the room and changes the channel.
Response:

1. You sit quietly and feel angry but don't decide to do anything.
2. You shout, 'Get away from the TV!'
3. You say, 'Excuse me I was watching my favourite TV show. It is just about over, and you'd be able to watch the other channel in a few minutes.'

Situation: Someone sits down beside you and blows smoke in your face.
Response:

1. You feel angry but don't say anything instead you get up and walk away.
2. You shout, 'Stop being such an ignorant clod, I can't stand cigarette smoke!'
3. You say, 'Excuse me, I would much prefer it if you didn't smoke beside me, it affects my breathing.'

Have the group members discuss how the responses differed from each other and what distinguished an assertive response from the others.

*Use index cards with a range of different situations listed on them, for example:

● You are looking for a specific item in the workshop and can't find it.

- Someone is sitting beside you and blowing smoke in your face.
- Someone has borrowed your shirt and not returned it.
- You have been late to group and the group leader has reprimanded you.
- Another patient has been swearing in front of you.
- You have been asked to clean the barbecue for three weeks in a row.

Have the group members divide into pairs, distribute the cards, and have them discuss between them how they think the situation should be responded to. They then decide between them how to role-play the situation and response. The group then rejoins and each pair role-plays to the rest of the group for feedback and discussion.

*Have some situations written on an index card that involve one person making a request of another, for example:

- Do you want to play billiards with me?
- I am going for a walk, would you like to go with me?
- I don't have any money. Could I borrow £1?
- I feel like playing cards. Are you interested in a game?
- I'm out of cigarettes. Can I have one?
- Could I have my meal with you tonight?

Have the group break up into pairs. Have one person refuse the request and one accept. They role-play this and then reverse roles. Bring it back to the group for role-play and discuss appropriate ways to make requests and how to be assertive and how to cope with refusal.

*Have situations relating to the person standing up for their rights written out on index cards, for example:

- You have bought a new dress and decide you don't like it and have to return it.
- You bought a shirt which is too tight and you need to exchange it.
- You have been waiting for a half-hour in a queue and someone pushes in ahead of you.
- You are standing at the counter waiting to be served, and other people are being served but not you.

- The cashier overcharges you for an item you have just bought.
- The coffee the waitress has given you is cold.

Have the group members break up into pairs, distribute the cards, have them discuss how to deal with the situation. Practice role-playing with both having a turn. Come back to the group for role-play in front of the group for feedback and general discussion.

*Have the group leader and co-leader role-play giving and receiving compliments. Then have the group members break up into pairs to practice giving and receiving compliments. Return to the group for further role-play, for feedback and for discussion concerning feelings related to giving and receiving compliments.

3. Homework assignments – The homework assignment is given out, explanations given as to what is required, and group members are asked to have completed it for the next session. An example of an assignment:

ASSERTIVENESS

Name: _____

Date: _____

Situation   What happened

_____

_____

_____

_____

_____

_____

Forensic Psychiatry for Health Professionals. Chris Lloyd. Published in 1995 by Chapman & Hall, London. ISBN 0 412 48350 5

4. Wrap-up – The sessions always conclude with the group leader recapitulating what have been the main points of the day's group, and asking for any feedback and comments.

Anger management

Aims: To teach alternative strategies of behaviour for dealing with a variety of behaviours. To teach group members to think before they react. To show that anger is a normal and healthy emotion, and that it can be resolved in a manner that does not progress to aggressive behaviours.

Media: handouts, whiteboard, anger journal, role-plays, discussion.

Structure of the group:
1. Introduction – The group leaders introduce themselves and briefly explain the outline and structure of the group, including the guidelines for the group, for example, no physical violence. Stress that group members will need to practice what is learnt in the session and feedback what has been taking place outside the group. Each group member introduces themselves and say what it is they'd like to gain or work on from today's group.

2. Discussion/activity – Anger is a complex and confusing feeling for many people. In order for people to better control a feeling like anger it needs first to be understood. The group leader, therefore, focuses on the following:

- defining anger;
- the nature of anger and how it affects people;
- increasing awareness as to the types of situations which arouse anger;
- methods of regulating and controlling anger, and
- better ways of dealing with situations that arouse anger.

The group sessions could be organized in the following way:

- Look at how each group member defines anger at the present time, and how that anger is expressed. Hand out work sheet on Anger for group members to fill in.

ANGER

Name: _____

Date: _____

What is your definition of anger? _____

How is your anger expressed? _____

Forensic Psychiatry for Health Professionals. Chris Lloyd. Published in 1995 by Chapman & Hall, London. ISBN 0 412 48350 5

Discuss how these questions were answered. Look at a working definition of anger, that is, it's an emotional reaction to certain types of stress and different from aggression, which is an action intended to cause injury or harm.

Give out the homework assignment: Keep an Anger Journal. In the journal each group member is asked to keep a record of their anger, the times they are angry and in what type of situation.

*Discuss why anger can become a problem, for example, stress, aggression, disturbed personal and social and work relationships.

Hand out worksheet 'When my anger has led to problems' for group members to fill in.

WHEN MY ANGER HAS LED TO PROBLEMS

Name: _____

Date: _____

Describe some situations in which your anger has led to problems. What happened?

_____

_____

Forensic Psychiatry for Health Professionals. Chris Lloyd. Published in 1995 by Chapman & Hall, London. ISBN 0 412 48350 5

Discuss the types of situations that were described. Are there any common situations or feelings? Write them up on the whiteboard.

Role-play some of the situations mentioned (without actually resorting to violence). Ask for feedback from group members about what they observed, for example, gestures, facial expression, posture, tone of voice and content of what was said.

Homework assignment: Practice keeping a handle on your anger if a similar situation arises that was talked about in today's group.

*Discuss what causes anger, referring to themes that have already been identified in previous sessions, for example, frustration, being put down, abuse, tension, maintaining a reputation, peer pressure, the need to dominate and exploitation.

Discuss what alternatives may have been available instead of responding violently.

The group leaders role-play (modelling) a number of alternative strategies for the situations group members had described.

The group members then role-play the situation that is most pertinent to them, trying out the alternative behaviour/attitude. The other members of the group give feedback of their observations.

Homework assignment: Ask the group members to observe someone around them over the next week who became angry: what was the situation? what happened? how did they think it could have been handled differently?

*Discuss messages about anger. Have the group members fill in the handout 'What I learnt about anger while growing up'.

WHAT I LEARNT ABOUT ANGER WHILE GROWING UP

Name: _____

Date: _____

How did your mother behave when she was angry?

_____

How did you know she was angry?

_____

How did your father behave when he was angry?

_____

How did you know he was angry? _____

How did your brother or sister behave when they were angry? _____

How did you know when they were angry?

_____

How did someone you most admire behave when they were angry? _____

How did you know when they were angry?

_____

How did you behave when you were angry?

_____

What responses did you get from people around you when you were angry? _____

Forensic Psychiatry for Health Professionals. Chris Lloyd. Published in 1995 by Chapman & Hall, London. ISBN 0 412 48350 5

Group members share what they have written. The group leader writes down the behaviours on the board. Are there any common themes or observations? How like/unlike are they to the people that were most significant to them?

Homework assignment: A situation during the week where the person was able to handle the situation that was making them feel angry.

*Have a further discussion on recognizing anger – this time look more specifically at how an individual's body feels when he is angry and how does he behave. Have group members fill in the handout 'Anger Signals'.

ANGER SIGNALS

Name: _____

Date: _____

When I am feeling angry my body feels _____

When I am angry I behave by _____

Forensic Psychiatry for Health Professionals. Chris Lloyd. Published in 1995 by Chapman & Hall, London. ISBN 0 412 48350 5

Group members share what they have written. Highlight the importance of recognizing body signals, that is, knowing when you are angry, and exactly what has made you angry: how will you deal with it, for example, go for a walk, hit the punching bag, take some deep breaths, give yourself positive self-talk?

Role-play their homework assignment, receive comments and feedback from other group members.

Homework assignment: Practice coping strategies in situations when you are feeling angry.

*Discuss the importance of understanding feelings. What happens for the individual, also for the other person in a confrontational scene. Look at coping strategies.

Look at the use of self-statements as a way of preventing angry feelings from escalating, for example, 'If I find I'm getting upset, I'll know how to handle it, 'Stay calm', 'My muscles are tightening, try to relax' and so on. Self-statements can be used to defuse the feelings of anger.

Have group members suggest other self-statements and write them up on the board. The group members can take a note of them. Discuss what sort of strategies have been working for them. Encourage sharing of ideas with other group members.

Homework assignment: Have group members practice using self-statements in a variety of situations when they are feeling angry.

In addition to the ideas presented, a number of additional sessions could be included on dealing with more specific examples of handling potentially angry situations, for example, handling peer group pressure, dealing with criticism, taking orders, being let down. Also, relaxation therapy and mental imagery are useful to include in conjunction with the anger management programme.

SUMMARY

This chapter has looked at a number of different programme options to help people learn how to behave in a more socially appropriate and acceptable manner.

RESOURCES

Hopson, B. and Scally, M. (1980) *Lifeskills Teaching Programmes*, Lifeskills Associates, Leeds.

Hughes, P. and Mullins, L. (1981) *Acute Psychiatric Care*, Charles B. Slack, Thorofare, N.J.

Wilkinson, J. and Canter, S. (1982) *Social Skills Training Manual*, John Wiley and Sons, Chichester.

REFERENCES

Drew, N. (1991) Combating the social isolation of chronic mental illness. *Journal of Psychosocial Nursing*, **29**, 14-7.

Folts, D. (1988) Social skills training, in *Occupational Therapy in Mental Health*, (eds D. Scott and N. Katz), Taylor and Francis, London, pp. 144-56.

Shelton, J. and Levy, R. (1981) *Behavioral Assignments and Treatment Compliance*, Research Press, Champaign, Illinois.

11

Leisure planning

INTRODUCTION

Institutionalized individuals spend most of their time being inactive. There is a lack of physical activity and of creativity. There needs to be an emphasis on developing effective personal use of available free time. The health professional needs to determine previous leisure patterns and interests and to focus on assisting the individual to acquire new leisure interests and skills.

This chapter aims to acquaint the health professional with the concept of leisure and the important role it plays in promoting wellness and personal growth for the individual. The process of providing a leisure planning service is examined, emphasizing the necessity for assessment before being able to develop and implement programmes. This chapter explores:

- concepts of leisure
- service-related difficulties
- assessment and
- programme planning.

For a health-promoting life, people require a balance in their lives between their work, self-maintenance and leisure activities. Before institutionalization, many forensic psychiatric clients lacked balance and routine in their lives. Then with institutionalization the institutional setting itself creates secondary difficulties by the very nature of the structure inherent in institutional life. As this compounds the situation for the forensic psychiatric client, it is essential to provide them with the opportunity to develop more structure in their lives and to establish more meaningful routines and roles for themselves.

Parry (1991) suggests that since many forensic psychiatric clients will have difficulty in obtaining full-time employment after leaving the institution, it is necesary to provide them with useful activities to carry out in their daily lives. Focusing on how to make effective use of leisure time enables the forensic psychiatric client to develop new interests, to add more meaning to daily life and to interact with others.

CONCEPTS OF LEISURE

Leisure is often viewed as free time; the time that is left over from work and other responsibilities that the individual has. This time is then used according to the individual's judgement or choice. The preference for involvement in certain kinds of leisure pursuits depends upon the individual's personality and life experiences. There are many leisure options available but unless the individual has been exposed to them, it is not so likely that they will be selected. People have a tendency to try things that they are more familiar with. Additionally, people tend to select leisure experiences in which they can expect a reasonable level of success. Past experiences and past success result in the individual expecting continued success in that particular leisure choice.

The perceptions, attitudes, feelings and needs of the individual and the meanings that people attribute to leisure determine the types of leisure pursuits that are followed. They may be solitary, involved with others, competitive, relaxing and so on. There is a dynamic interaction between a given individual and other individuals, groups, environmental or cultural elements. In addition, social, psychological, economic, cultural, personal and environmental variables all have a part to play in the leisure choices made by individuals. What is important is what takes place for the individual while engaging in the activity.

Lack of leisure pursuits

For mentally ill people, leisure may have little meaning since it is frequently the case that they have an abundance of non-obligated time. They have deficits in their daily living skills and in social and leisure involvement which increases their inability to engage in meaningful life experiences. Champney and Dzurec (1992) suggest that a typical pattern for these people consists of sitting around with nothing to do most of the time, not being busy, having a hard time getting out of bed, no spending money or transportation, no opportunities for jobs, school or social activities, unhappy with personal accomplishments, bored and lonely. They have few competence-enhancing or mastery experiences. Because of this they are less inclined to attempt anything different to what they are accustomed to. This leads to their leading a very unbalanced life where their daily activities are narrow in scope and unrewarding.

Personal competence

Howe-Murphy and Charboneau (1987) found that an increase in the perceived personal control of institutionalized individuals enhanced their activeness, interpersonal activity, mental alertness and psychological well-being. They also found that increased personal competence resulting from the attainment of new leisure skills seems to enhance self-concept. Iso-Ahola (1984) found that enhanced perceived freedom and control increased institutionalized individuals activity levels in general and their interpersonal activity in particular.

Dowd (1984) suggests that the health care professional providing a leisure service should emphasize increased awareness of competence-enhancing experiences and actual participation in competence-enhancing activities to aid in developing an individual's sense of mastery and control. This is an important concept since many people fail in their attempts to adjust to community living as a result of inappropriate use of their leisure time.

Environment

Certain environments used by the institutionalized person have a number of effects. The environment may advance or hinder the efforts of the individual to progress or cope. Many institutional environments, especially in maximum security settings or the large institutions for the mentally ill, are crowded, poorly designed, lack decorations that are pleasing to the eye, and furniture and equipment may be old and in poor repair.

Research has shown that environmental factors such as aesthetics influence psychological attitude (Howe-Murphy and Charboneau, 1987). A physically supportive design encourages positive interactions and is pleasing to the senses. Additionally, it is important to provide an emotionally supportive environment which then encourages openness, trust, risk taking, social interactions and caring. It is important to help people utilize leisure activities to enrich their total pattern of interaction with the environment (Blocher and Siegal, 1984).

The degree to which an individual adapts to the environment is closely related to the types and levels of their adaptive skills. Each client has the right to be exposed to opportunities to develop, rehearse, perfect and re-learn skills for daily living of which leisure is an integral part. It is only then that the individual should assume responsibility for identifying desirable life directions and leisure experiences (Tinsley and Tinsley, 1984).

Wellness and personal growth

Leisure has an important influence on the mental health and life satisfaction of the individual (McDowell, 1984). A sense of personal stability and continuity needs to be gained. This can be achieved depending upon the extent to which the individual uses leisure to fulfil his needs. According to Tinsley and Tinsley (1984), individuals should be able to use their leisure to raise self-esteem, increase life satisfaction and facilitate self-actualization.

Leisure is important for providing meaning to life. Satisfaction with leisure experiences adds to the perceived quality of life. Higher levels of involvement in leisure and free-time activities are associated with higher ratings of overall well-being and life satisfaction. Champney and Dzurec (1992) suggest that an intervention directed at getting clients involved in activities of their own choosing and matching their skills and needs would result in much greater improvements in satisfaction over time.

Powell and Sable (1990) advocate the benefits associated with empowering the client to take an active role in the healing process since each person has a level of self-responsibility for their own health. Involvement in leisure is a means of minimizing the distress of illness and of encouraging the client to work towards recovery. Leisure experiences provide one of the few opportunities in the lives of most individuals to engage in exploratory and creative activity, where the end result is a satisfying process rather than an end product.

To find meaning in life there needs to be a sense of connectedness of the past, present and future. The integration of one's physical, mental, emotional, spiritual and social status are important in the concept of wellness. It is affected by nutrition, events in one's life, the nature of one's work, play and living environment, including aesthetics, cleanliness and interpersonal relationships. The therapist needs to emphasize intact strengths and provide activities and leisure experiences that are meaningful.

Hilyer and associates (1982) found that physical fitness training elevates low self-esteem, reduces anxiety and depression, and, in general, promotes a healthier psychological state.

SERVICE-RELATED DIFFICULTIES

In the maximum security environment the health professional is faced by a population that characteristically exhibit low self-esteem, fear and distrust, and backgrounds of assaultive, hostile behaviour which necessitates special security precautions (Jewell, 1977). This then restricts the options available to the health professional. Depending on institutional regulations, clients may not be allowed to use anything that has the potential to be used as a weapon, for example scissors, baseball bats.

Leisure has been supported as an important feature in maximum security settings but traditionally it has been used to alleviate boredom or to fill in time (Munson, 1991). The types of leisure options are usually limited and tend to focus on exercise programmes which are carried out in a large group. Orton (1977) concluded that recreational activities are not being nurtured.

Another problem in service delivery relates to the attitude of institutional staff. For some of these staff, they view leisure as a privilege rather than a right. This then leads to their being obstructive when leisure activities are being planned and organized.

The actual environment may not be conducive to conducting leisure programmes. In some facilities there is limited available space or the space that has been allocated may not be very conducive to a pleasant leisure experience.

Being in an institution has an impact on the residents. Regimentation, lack of privacy, limited contact with family and friends, limited opportunities for decision-making and a relative scarcity of goods and services do not encourage independent leisure choices or participation.

Strategies

Before implementing a leisure programme it is essential to sell the idea. This can be accomplished in a number of ways:

- Seek the support of the facility administrator.
- Provide inservice education to the staff.
- Have a thorough knowledge of leisure principles.
- Develop a resource package with a wide range of options.
- Establish links with the community.
- Design and present a programme that clearly demonstrates what you hope to achieve.
- Actively solicit input from staff members concerning what they see as the residents' needs.
- Encourage the staff to evaluate the programme's effectiveness.

Leisure principles

Stumbo and Little (1991) suggest a number of principles for providing leisure programming in the secure setting. Leisure services should:

- be based on rehabilitation principles;
- be viewed as a right not a privilege;
- focus on the residents' return to the community;
- take into account the residents' cultural background;
- be tailored to individual needs wherever possible;
- provide for individual and inroom activities;
- promote choice, freedom and control and self-responsibility; and
- provide a variety of outlets for residents.

ASSESSMENT

Before developing a leisure programme, it is necessary to conduct an individualized leisure assessment. The assessment should cover such areas as leisure attitudes, leisure skills and leisure behaviours or patterns as well as any constraints or barriers that may interfere with the client engaging in success-ful leisure experiences (Howe, 1984).

Trevan-Hawke (1985) suggests that in the initial assess-ment a number of features should be incorporated, such as: time and money available to the client, occupation, level of education, car ownership, stage in life cycle, demo-graphic/geographic details, and traditional and current attitudes to leisure. The data that has been collected can then be used as a guide in the provision of service to the client.

The assessment process looks at leisure-related problem-solving, leisure awareness, leisure resource guidance and leisure skills development. A leisure programme helps the client to become involved in leisure experiences that are intrinsically meaningful, satisfying and personally effective.

A number of the clients seen fall into the special needs group. This is particularly important when assessing people from different racial and cultural groups. One has to consider their customs, rites, rituals, roles, traditions, expectations and views.

Assessment instruments

There are a number of assessment instruments available, including:

Leisure Attitude Scale (Ragheb, 1980).
Survey of Leisure Values (Loesch, 1980).
Comprehensive Evaluation in Recreation Therapy Scale (Parker *et al.*, 1975).
Leisure Satisfaction Scale (Beard and Ragheb, 1980).
Leisure Activity Blank (McKechnie, 1975).
Value Systems (Hughes and Mullins, 1981).
The Interest Checklist (Matsutsuyu, 1969).

PROGRAMME PLANNING

In running a leisure programme, both individual or group strategies may be employed. Leisure education should focus on meaningful activities that promote awareness, responsibility, independence, skills development, decision-making and resource awareness. The key goal is to try and establish new and appropriate leisure interests and behaviour so that the institutionalized clients will make successful transitions to the community, and, once there, maintain satisfying leisure lifestyles.

Leisure programmes on a group basis can be organized in six- to eight-week blocks. It is necessary to write up the objectives and aims of the programme to present to other staff members. Writing up a programme register or plan for each new group programme keeps the lines of communication open with other team members. Additionally, it gives the therapist enough time to plan ahead, to make sure of availability of resources and to involve outside agencies/volunteers if necessary.

Warren (1993) suggests that protocols are extremely important when designing programmes. By utilizing a protocol format, intentions can be explained by providing concise information about what will be done, to whom, by whom, and how. The benefit of this approach is that a detailed document is prepared for seeking approval for service developments, negotiating resources or contracts of service, and assists in providing continuity of care.

AN EXAMPLE OF A LEISURE PROGRAMME PROTOCOL

Group programme: Creative Leisure Group

Objective:

To introduce clients to activities that provide some meaning and satisfaction in their lives.

Aims:

- Learn new leisure activities.
- Have the opportunity for creative self-expression.

- Have the opportunity to socialize with other people.
- Have the opportunities to learn about leisure resources in the community.

Referral:

Any clients who are seen as requiring the development of leisure skills, and who are not actively unwell.

Intervention (plan/method):

Week 1 – Topic: Tie-dying t-shirts
  Method: Instruction, demonstration, practical experience.
Week 2 – Topic: Woodburning
  Method: Instruction, demonstration, practical experience.
Week 3 – Topic: Leisure in the community
  Method: Volunteer, brochures, discussion.
Week 4 – Topic: Planning and growing a herb garden
  Method: Discussion, potting plants.
Week 5 – Topic: Gift ideas
  Method: Discussion, making potpourri sachets, dried flower bookmarks, stationery.
Week 6 – Topic: Folk art
  Method: Instruction and group activity.
Week 7 – Topic: Art
  Method: Discussion, practical experience using different media such as paints, crayon, charcoal.
Week 8 – Topic: Special events project.
  Method: Group activity, for example, making Christmas decorations.

Location and Time:

Craft room #1 Tuesday and Thursday 2.00 to 3.30

Liaison:

Occupational therapist and psychiatric nurse plus community volunteers.

Outcomes:

Administration of the Leisure Checklist after group sessions.

Leisure checklist

To chart the progress of the group and whether group members are making gains by being involved in the programme, a quick Leisure Checklist can be administered after each session. This will assist the facilitator in making any changes to the group format that may be required. It will provide a baseline about where people currently are in developing leisure skills and knowledge of resources.

LEISURE CHECKLIST

Name: _____

Date: _____

Please circle the appropriate response.

1. Do you have a hobby that you can do on a regular basis?   Yes   No
2. Have you ever attended a course?   Yes   No
3. Do you know what types of courses are available? Yes   No
4. Have you ever attended a cultural activity such as the theatre, museum or art gallery?   Yes   No
5. Do you ever go to any local sporting facilities, for example, swimming pool, gym?   Yes   No
6. Are you aware of the recreation facilities in your area, for example, parks, picnic grounds, reserves? Yes   No
7. Have you ever done the activity demonstrated in this group before?   Yes   No
8. Do you think you would be interested in doing this activity again?   Yes   No
9. Did you find doing this activity helped you to talk to other people in the group?   Yes   No

10. Are you interested in finding out further information
    about leisure options?   Yes   No
Any additional comments:

_____

_____

Forensic Psychiatry for Health Professionals. Chris Lloyd. Published in 1995 by Chapman & Hall, London. ISBN 0 412 48350 5

Programme Focus

Leisure programmes should focus on locating low-cost activities in the community, that can be done in the home or neighbourhood, and that focus on re-establishing social and family relationships. Incorporate using purposeful activities that have greater meaning and transferability into the home and community.

Individualization

Clients need to feel that their individual needs are being met. Beard and Ragheb (1980) mention a number of factors which individuals perceive as meeting satisfaction in their leisure choices, for example, psychological, educational, social, relaxational, physiological and aesthetic. This then encourages individuals to perceive themselves as having the potential to become independent, successful or self-directed. They are also then more likely to identify specific needs and values, select ways of attaining their leisure goals, and then experience a measure of success with resulting satisfaction.

Creative programming

The average person spends quite a bit of their leisure time in individual pursuits. The people seen in forensic facilities frequently have restrictions placed on them regarding access to tools or equipment. Depending on the type of facility, they may spend a lot of their time alone. Another consideration is that a lot of these people have limited funds. Past experiences were often not rewarding or satisfying and they often have the expectation of failure or of not being able to accomplish anything. Encouraging leisure pursuits that are achievable enable people to experience self-determination, self-expression and individuality.

Some examples of activities

There are a large number of activities that can be pursued. In the forensic system, it is important to encourage exposure to a variety of activities – from ones that can be done alone, to others that involve other people. As well as looking at activities that can be done while in the facility, it is necessary to look at other types of activities that can be carried out in the community, and, in the pre-discharge phase, to go into the community and try out some of these activities. People need support while engaging in new leisure pursuits and in becoming familiar with what is available in the community. Just informing people of what is available without practical exposure is unlikely to result in them actually trying them out. Some different types of leisure activities are listed below:

- Personal self expression:
  - writing poetry or short stories
  - creating children's games
  - drawing and sketching
  - keeping a diary
  - recording family history
  - writing a short play
  - writing children's stories

- Cottage interests:
  - baking bread
  - making pickles and chutneys
  - making jams and marmalades
  - growing herbs
  - making pot-pourri
  - growing vegetables
  - dried flower arrangements
  - drying herbs
  - making Christmas wreaths and table centre-pieces

- Quiet-time activities:
  - yoga
  - sewing/embroidery

- knitting
- crocheting
- weaving
- watching TV
- collecting stamps
- crosswords
- jigsaw puzzles
- patience
- reading books/magazines

- Cultural/educational:
  - museum
  - art gallery
  - pottery
  - arts and craft displays
  - library
  - taking a class
  - voluntary work
  - theatre
  - music

- Outdoor activities:
  - gardening
  - going for a picnic
  - having a barbecue
  - feeding the ducks
  - going for a walk
  - going bushwalking
  - visiting the park
  - visiting a plant nursery
  - going for a drive
  - birdwatching

- Creative:
  - woodcarving
  - woodburning
  - sculpture
  - pottery
  - jewellery making
  - weaving wallhangings
  - painting

- Sporting/social activities:
    - swimming
    - fishing
    - social dancing
    - pool/billiards
    - table tennis
    - darts
    - bingo
    - cycling
    - aerobics

Working with individual clients

The health professional is required to establish rapport with the client, explore the client's expectations and the nature of the problems being experienced, while helping the client develop a positive self-concept.

It is essential for the health professional to involve the individual in appropriate leisure choices and to facilitate development of positive feelings towards community living. People should be helped to satisfy their needs more flexibly and completely by becoming increasingly aware of their existing behaviour and attitudes, examining their time usage and changing their leisure attitudes and behaviours so that they have more success and satisfaction.

Case study

G. is a 56-year-old woman with a depressive illness. Her involvement with the legal system, assessment for a court report, was as a result of shoplifting. She was referred for leisure assessment since the ward staff were concerned about her isolative behaviour. The assessment revealed that she was widowed, had one son whom she was close to but had problems relating to her daughter-in-law, and she had two small granddaughters. She had always been a homemaker. She had no friends and did not go to church or pursue any social activities in the community. The leisure interests she described related to the past. These included knitting, baking, gardening and walking the dog. She did not know how to go about using public transport – if she needed driving anywhere her son did it for her – and was unaware of available leisure options and resources. She had difficulty structuring her day and described it as an endless blur where all she looked forward to was going to bed. She was unclear as to her values and needs concerning leisure and could not determine what she would like to try. Further discussion revealed that she had been very dependent on her husband and had greatly enjoyed that role; now that she was on her own, she just did not know what to do about meeting new people or going on her own to places in the community. After negotiation, it was decided that she would do some knitting for her granddaughters, join the bible group, take up reading magazines, look into the idea of volunteer work and have leisure counselling to help her work out how to restructure her day. In addition, she was referred to a community centre to help her with learning about the buses, about what resources were available in the community and in attending the day programme activities.

SUMMARY

This chapter explores the concept of leisure and suggests a process to follow when designing and implementing leisure programmes in secure settings.

FURTHER READING

Dowd, E. (1984) (ed.) *Leisure Counseling*, Charles C. Thomas, Springfield, Illinois.
Howe-Murphy, R. and Charboneau, B. (1987) *Therapeutic Recreation Intervention*, Prentice-Hall, Inc., Englewood Cliffs, N.J.

REFERENCES

Beard, J. and Ragheb, M. (1980) Measuring leisure satisfaction. *Journal of Leisure Research, First Quarter,* 20–32.
Blocher, D. and Siegal, R. (1984) Towards a cognitive developmental

theory of leisure and work, in *Leisure Counseling. Concepts and Applications*, (ed. E. Dowd), Charles C. Thomas, Springfield, Illinois, pp. 52–79.

Champney, T. and Dzurec, L. (1992) Involvement in productive activities and satisfaction with living situation among severely mentally disabled adults. *Hospital and Community Psychiatry*, **43**, 899–903.

Dowd, E. (1984) Leisure counseling with adults across the life span, in *Leisure Counseling. Concepts and Applications*, (ed. E. Dowd), Charles C. Thomas, Springfield, Illinois, pp. 214–33.

Hilyer, J., Wilson, D., Dillon, C. *et al.* (1982) Physical fitness training and counseling as treatment for youthful offenders. *Journal of Counseling Psychology*, **29**, 292–303.

Howe, C. (1984) Leisure assessment and counseling, in *Leisure Counseling. Concepts and Applications*, (ed. E. Dowd), Charles C. Thomas, Springfield, Illinois, pp. 234–53.

Howe-Murphy, R. and Charboneau, B. (1987) *Therapeutic Recreation Intervention. An Ecological Perspective*, Prentice–Hall, Inc., Englewood Cliffs, N.J.

Hughes, P. and Mullins, L. (1981) *Acute Psychiatric Care*, Charles B. Slack, Inc., Thorofare, N.J.

Iso-Ahola, S. (1984) Social psychological foundations of leisure and resultant implications for leisure counseling, in *Leisure Counseling. Concepts and Applications*, (ed. E. Dowd), Charles C. Thomas, Springfield, Illinois, pp. 97–125.

Jewell, D. (1977) Maximum security: Some obstacles of meaningful recreational programing. *Therapeutic Recreation Journal*, **11**, 184–8.

Loesch, L. (1980) *Leisure Counseling*, Eric/Caps, Ann Arbor, Michigan.

Matsutsuyu, J. (1969) The interest checklist. *American Journal of Occupational Therapy*, **23**, 323–8.

McDowell, C. (1984) Leisure: Consciousness, well-being, and counseling, in *Leisure Counseling. Concepts and Applications*, (ed. E. Dowd), Charles C. Thomas, Springfield, Illinois, pp. 5–51.

McKechnie, G. (1975) *Manual for the Leisure Activities Blank*, Consulting Psychologists Press, Palo Alto, California.

Munson, W. (1991) Juvenile delinquency as a societal problem and social disability: The therapeutic recreator's role as ecological change agent. *Therapeutic Recreation Journal*, **25**, 19–30.

Orton, D. (1977) An investigation of the past, present, and future recreation pursuits of adult inmates in two Iowa correctional institutions. *Therapeutic Recreation Journal*, **11**, 66–9.

Parker, R., Ellison, C., Kirby, T. *et al.* (1975) Comprehensive evaluation in recreation therapy scale: A tool for patient evaluation. *Therapeutic Recreation Journal, Fourth Quarter*, 143–53.

Parry, J. (1991) Community care for mentally ill offenders. *Nursing Standard*, **5**, 29–33.

Powell, L. and Sable, J. (1990) Application of holistic health techniques in therapeutic recreation. *Therapeutic Recreation Journal*, **24**, 32–41.

Ragheb, M. (1980) Interrelationships among leisure participation, leisure satisfaction, and leisure attitudes. *Journal of Leisure Research, Second Quarter,* 138–49.

Stumbo, N. and Little, S. (1991) Implications for leisure services with incarcerated women. *Therapeutic Recreation Journal,* **25,** 49–62.

Tinsley, H. and Tinsley, D. (1984) Leisure counseling models, in *Leisure Counseling. Concepts and Applications,* (ed. E. Dowd), Charles C. Thomas, Springfield, Illinois, pp. 80–96.

Trevan-Hawke, J. (1985) Occupational therapy and the role of leisure. *British Journal of Occupational Therapy,* **48,** 299–301.

Warren, I. (1993) Introduction to protocols for occupational therapy. *British Journal of Occupational Therapy,* **56,** 25–7.

12

Preparation for the community

INTRODUCTION

After a period of being institutionalized, individuals are typically anxious and concerned about how they are going to manage in the community. They may well have had past experiences in the community which were neither satisfying nor productive and may fear returning to an environment where they were not successful. There needs to be a focus on activities that promote acquisition of skills necessary for independent community living. A key aim of discharge programmes is facilitating a smooth transition from the institutional environment to the community.

This chapter aims to look at the types of programmes that can be developed which focus on specific tasks and skills required to manage the forensic psychiatric client's life competently. These types of programmes require accurate problem identification, goal setting, didactic input, experiential learning and exposure to community resources and options. This chapter explores:

- treatment planning
- goal-setting and
- discharge programmes.

TREATMENT PLANNING

The overall goal of discharge preparation is to restore and/or maintain the clients' capacity to function in the community.

There are a unique set of problems associated with mentally ill clients who have been institutionalized in a secure setting. These clients have functional performance deficits that complicate their illness. Programmes are directed towards building on the strengths of the clients to help them reach their maximum potential for successful independent living. Clients need to be provided with a therapeutic environment which encourages competency and mastery of necessary life tasks and skills. In addition, there are a number of other agencies that play an important part in the rehabilitation of the forensic psychiatric client. Voluntary organizations offer services such as accommodation, advice, support or simply a place to go in the evenings. Probation officers provide much of the assistance for discharged forensic psychiatric clients directed towards helping them cope in the community. It is important to foster these links since forensic clients require a particularly high level of care and supervision upon return to the community.

Frequently, clients who are discharged have a wide range of problems. They often tend to be undereducated, under-skilled and socially isolated (Hochberger and Fisher-James, 1992). They may have the skills and abilities to establish full independent living but their ability to achieve this may be influenced by other factors: lack of support network, poor social skills, poor daily living skills and poor problem-solving ability. The overall impact is to reduce the client's capacity to succeed in specific areas.

This situation of multifaceted problems is intensified in clients who experience a chronic disability and extended periods of institutionalization in a secure setting. The capacity of such clients to deal with their problems is reduced by extended exclusion from the community and from maintaining independent living (Cohen *et al.*, 1980).

Both individual and group programmes may be designed to assist mentally abnormal clients to progress from their present level of functioning to their needed level of functioning. Clients are assisted in acquiring the skills necessary to advance from where they are to where they need to be (Anthony *et al.*, 1980).

Programmes use specific therapeutic interventions that are meant to facilitate the attainment of the identified goals.

However, merely identifying and/or defining goals do not necessarily mean that the client will attain these goals. The initial problem and the established goal has to be personally relevant for the client.

Problem identification

One useful way of looking at problem identification and subsequent goal setting is to break the process down into three stages:

- exploration
- understanding and
- action.

This involves an interactive process/relationship between the health professional and client with the emphasis being on working through what is of most personal relevance to the client.

Carkhuff and Berenson (1977) suggest that client learning involves three phases – exploration of where they are in relation to their world, their understanding of where they want or need to be, and finally, the action required to achieve where they want to be.

Exploration by the client is a key element in the therapeutic process. The initial contact and development of the process of exploration enables both the health professional and the client to gain an understanding of where the client is at present.

In order to gain this understanding, the client needs to be able to move beyond the exploratory phase. Understanding occurs when the client knows or understands him or herself. The material that has been explored needs to be built on in order for the client to look at where they would like to be. In this manner the individual is encouraged to take ownership of the problems that have been explored/identified.

Once clients have taken ownership of their problems and feelings, they are in the position to make a decision to act upon them. The health professional guides the client in developing a relevant course of action. Observing the clients and their behaviour and actions will give the health professional an idea about the clients' weaknesses and resources.

The health professional must respond to both the content and feeling of what the client is talking about. The client may talk about a problem but may not share their feelings about the problem. Further exploration provides a basis for client personalizing which promotes self-understanding.

The meaning of the problem, feelings and goal need to be personalized which leads to accountability. Being accountable leads to the formulation of goals that are specifically relevant to the client.

The goal that is established must be concrete and have observable, measurable steps. The health professional assists the client in working out an action plan. This involves an interactive process between the health professional and client. One such method of devising an action plan is that of Goal Attainment Scaling.

GOAL-SETTING

Goal Attainment Scaling (GAS) was first developed by Kiresuk and Sherman (1968) as a programme evaluation tool. Since that time it has been widely written about and used in a variety of ways.

The client and health professional mutually decide upon a realistic set of goals to work on. For each goal specified, a scale composed of a graded series of likely treatment outcomes is established ranging from least to most favourable. Descriptions on each point should be precise, objective and observable. These points are assigned numerical values: -2 for a least favourable outcome, $+2$ for a most favourable outcome, with the value 0 assigned to the treatment outcome most likely (Kiresuk and Sherman, 1968).

It is important that the scale points be stated in terms of events, the presence or absence of which can be easily observed.

A set of weights may also be specified for the goals, reflecting the relative value of each goal as an indicator of successful treatment.

The goals are stated in measurable behaviours. Small, achievable goals have a greater chance of success. Being successful reinforces the client's attempts to keep working towards attaining the overall goal.

GOAL ATTAINMENT SCALING			
	Scale 1	Scale 2	Scale 3
	Goal Weights		
Outcome Value			
Most unfavourable treatment outcome thought likely (− 2)			
Less than expected success with treatment (− 1)			
Expected level of Treatment success (0)			
More than expected success with treatment (+ 1)			
Best anticipated treatment success (+ 2)			

Forensic Psychiatry for Health Professionals. Chris Lloyd. Published in 1995 by Chapman & Hall, London. ISBN 0 412 48350 5

The goals need to be the client's. The more the client is aware that they have set their own concrete, realistic goals, the higher the degree of commitment and identification with them (Herje, 1980).

Making a contract with the client, involving mutual goal-setting, is an effective way to achieve positive healthcare outcomes. Facilitating such active involvement of clients in their own treatment is an important part of the health professional's role (Herje, 1980).

GAS takes a position by stating what will be accomplished rather than what needs remedying (Choate *et al.*, 1981).

A somewhat different approach to using Goal Attainment Scaling was developed by psychology staff at South Carolina State Hospital. This is known as the Goal Attainment Scaling for Psychiatric Inpatients (GASPI) (Guy and Moore, 1982). They developed a new evaluation tool as they required a scale that could define the kinds of problems frequently encountered among a chronic institutionalized population. It is patterned after Kiresuk and Sherman's (1968) model yet designed to meet the needs of a chronic psychiatric population. Owing to the nature of the treatment setting, with emphasis on group therapy, the GASPI was designed to accommodate the problems encountered in these situations.

The uses of GASPI diverge from the uses of GAS. GAS is primarily used for goal-setting between client and therapist. GASPI can be used to identify client's current functioning levels, pinpoint the areas of need, and observation of patients at the end of a prescribed treatment period to determine their degree of progress.

The areas covered include: affect, aggression, attention-concentration, attention-seeking, body odour, clothing, concrete-abstract, co-operation (negativism), decisiveness, dependence-independence, direction following, directionality, egocentricity, emotional lability, empathy, energy level, eye contact, frustration tolerance, goal formulation, grooming, impulsivity, insight, interaction (quantitative), long-term memory, orientation to person, place, and time, participation, passivity, posture, responsibility, self-confidence, shaving, short-term memory, somatizing, suicidal talk, 'uh-uh' and qualitative and quantitative verbalization.

Guy and Moore (1982) outline the following reasons for considering using the GASPI:

- provides discrete behavioural indices to measure client's progress;
- pinpoints patients who may not be receiving appropriate care as indicated by their GASPI scores (e.g. unrealistic goal, unsuitable therapeutic intervention);

- determines whether clients benefit from specific treatment programmes;
- assists in decision-making if the client has maintained the desired level for a specified period of time to discontinue therapy;
- establishes treatment programmes that are according to the clients' functioning levels;
- re-allocates resources to programmes that are most likely to produce the desired results;
- improves communication between caregivers since preset behavioural objectives allow treatment providers to speak a common language, and
- assists novice therapists' thinking to form reasonable goals for therapeutic intervention.

DISCHARGE PROGRAMMES

Discharge programmes vary considerably depending on the type of facility, length of institutionalization, diagnosis, resources available, and the availability, expertise and orientation of the health professionals.

A number of studies have been conducted looking at the types of issues that are important to focus on in providing discharge preparation. Some of these issues include housing, leisure, isolation, support networks and medication.

Results of a study by Champney and Dzurec (1992) indicate that when clients are appropriately housed, satisfaction with their living situation may be involved by their participation in meaningful activities. They suggest that higher levels of involvement in leisure and free-time activities are associated with higher ratings of overall well-being and life satisfaction.

The chronically mentally ill are often excluded from ordinary social interactions that provide opportunities to develop their social self (Drew, 1991). They are often lonely and isolated and report sitting around with nothing to do (Champney and Dzurec, 1992).

Chronically mentally ill people have disabilities that transcend and complicate their illness. These include:

- primary disability – lethargy, odd and unacceptable

behaviour, lack of awareness of handicaps, and disturbances in social relationships;

- secondary disability – wariness, avoidance, withdrawal and refusal to accept the limitations of illness, and
- tertiary disability – diminished social networks, stigma, poverty, unemployment and a general lack of belonging.

Bachrach (1986) urges for the design of multifaceted programmes to respond to the wide variety of treatment needs.

Robinson and Pinkey (1992) suggest the importance of using a problem-solving approach which provides opportunities for patients to make decisions and assume responsibility for their own lives. Mohr (1993) also stresses the importance of empowering the mentally ill client. This involves restoring the individual's self-confidence and dignity in order to improve their quality of life.

Harmon and Tratnack (1992) stress the need to encourage active participation in treatment and to focus on client strengths rather than deficits. Without adequate preparation for community roles, most clients have been unsuccessful in their adjustment to the community. Peterson (1986) highlights the need for *in vivo* training in the outside community so that the newly learned skills are maintained. Increasing the individual's exposure to the community and promoting the use of resources outside the hospital are important (Robinson and Pinkey, 1992).

Clients' comprehension of what medication has been prescribed and when and why they are to take it has been found to be very low (Clary *et al.*, 1992). They suggest that clinicians are not doing the job as effectively as they could be. The end result will inevitably be treatment non-compliance with a consequent increase in relapse and rehospitalization. The importance of medication management in discharge preparation is that clients increased knowledge of their treatment regimen is generally associated with higher levels of adherence to prescribed medication (Clary *et al.*, 1992; Mohr, 1993).

Research suggests that simply being aware of client needs and making referrals to community resources following discharge to meet these needs are not enough (Cohen *et al.*, 1980). Despite the fact that almost all forms of outpatient psychiatric treatment provided to clients after hospital discharge prevent relapse and rehospitalization, the rate of compliance with aftercare follow-up is disturbingly low (Axelrod and Wetzler, 1989). It has been found that clients fail to understand the need for the resource, have anxiety about the stigma attached to utilization of the resource and about approaching the resource to receive benefits. Increased after-care compliance has been found to be associated with continuity of care between the hospital and the community resource (Axelrod and Wetzler, 1989).

AN EXAMPLE OF A DISCHARGE PREPARATION PROGRAMME

Discharge preparation group

The discharge preparation group focuses on six areas that are thought to be important in assisting the client to verbalize concerns about discharge, increasing awareness of what they need to do for themselves to survive in the community, and of increasing awareness of community resources and options.

The discharge preparation group covers the following areas:

- finding a place to live (accommodation)
- getting from one place to another (transportation)
- taking care of oneself (medication, nutrition, fitness)
- discharge situations (concerns, thoughts, feelings)
- connection with others (leisure, meeting people) and
- community services/resources (follow-up).

Each group's content consists of introduction, discussion, didactic input and experiential learning. Didactic teaching without an experiential component has been found not to be successful in increasing self-esteem and confidence in exploring new possibilities (Versluys, 1980).

The group sessions all follow a similar format: introduction, explanation as to the purpose of the group, activity, discussion and wrap-up. Following are some examples of how the various sessions making up the discharge preparation group can be organized.

Accommodation

Aim: To increase awareness of the means that can be used to find available accommodation.

Media: map of the local community, local newspaper, pens, paper, board.

Activity/discussion:

1. Divide the group up into subgroups with a map and a newspaper. The task is: 'find a suitable place to live'. Get them to make notes about the reason for their selection. Rejoin the group for discussion, each subgroup explaining why they have chosen a particular area. Points made should be listed on the board. Did people list similar reasons? Discussion should focus on specific issues such as:

- convenience of housing to community services, e.g. shops, transport, clinic, cost;
- type of housing, e.g. boarding house, flat, hostel, shared accommodation, and
- other options for finding accommodation, e.g. going to a real estate agency, by asking social services for assistance, asking friends for recommendations.

2. Role-play: 'Looking at accommodation'. Include: Explaining to the landlord that you're seeking accommodation, asking what is included, how much will it cost, any specific rules and regulations that have to be observed, what is the bond, how much notice is required if one has to move. Have all patients practice the role-play and have feedback and discussion.

3. Discussion: 'Have you had any housing problems in the past?' Write list of problems on the board. Take each problem individually. Ask group members can they think of ways the problem could have been handled. List alternatives. Look at what community resources might have been able to prevent or resolve the problem. Have group members look up in the phonebook the numbers of differing types of community agencies that may be useful, for example, local community centre, social services, St. Vincent de Paul.

4. Field excursion: Have the clients look at a map of the local area and decide which area they would like to go to. Use public transport to have a look at the local area. Visit such community services as St. Vincent de Paul, Salvation Army, community rental agencies.

Transportation

Aim: To increase awareness of the different types of transport in the community and how to use them.

Media: map of the local area, bus timetable, train timetable, phonebook, pens, paper, fieldtrip.

Activity:

1. Discussion on different types of transportation. How do members of the group travel around their community? What are some of the factors involved, for example, cost, convenience, distance, time. What are alternative to public transportation, for example, taxi, hitching, walking, bicycle. How do members feel about using public transport? Have they experienced any difficulties? What types of difficulties?

2. Activity: 'Do we know the local area?' Divide the group up into teams. Look at map with key places marked on it. Do they know how to get to where is marked? Use a phonebook to look up the phone number of the bus company, then phone to find out the bus route, time of departure, how often the buses run, and cost. Come back to the group and discuss the results of what they have found.

3. Divide the group into pairs. Give each pair a different time that they have to meet the train. Have each pair work out what they need to do to be able to catch the train on time, for example, it's a late train, and there's no bus, have to catch a taxi, find out taxi phone number, phone taxi and find out approximate cost to the station. When everyone has worked out a solution bring it back to the group for discussion – were they all realistic, well thought out, practical?

4. Have group members decide where they'd like to go in the community. Plan the bus route; find out the time to catch the bus. Go for a field trip on the bus to the selected destination. Then go on from there to visit the train station. This activity may need to be repeated a number of times in order for people to become more comfortable and familiar with using public transport.

Medication

Aim: To increase awareness of the need to know more about the medication that one is taking.

Media: Pens, paper, board, guest speaker, film.

Activity:

1. Administer a brief questionnaire asking: Do you know what medication you are taking? Can you name the medication you are taking? What time do you take your medication? What dose are you taking? Do you know why you are taking this medication?
Discuss how the group members feel about taking medications and what their concerns are.

2. Present a guest speaker (or film) to look at the major groupings of medication, the types of symptom relief they provide, what types of side effects, duration of taking medication. Answer any queries.

3. Discuss the importance of taking medication: what do you do if you miss taking some of your medication? who can you call to talk to about your medication?

4. As people in the group near discharge, they should assume more responsibility for taking medication. They should be encouraged to ask for their medication specifically to increase their own responsibility for medication.

Nutrition

Aim: To learn about the importance of eating the right food to feel well.

Media: Board, food group chart, magazines, scissors, glue, food.

Activity:

1. Discuss the importance of good nutrition. Review the food group chart. Have group members talk about the routine of how they eat, and the types of food they eat.

2. Write out the basic food groups on a large sheet of paper. Hand around magazines and have the group members cut out pictures of food from the different food groups and paste them onto their sheets of paper. Ask the group members in turn to show their selection and have a discussion on what they have chosen.

3. Have group members discuss what makes a balanced meal plan for a day. Write up on the board suggested meal plans and discuss how meals can be more nutritious. Hand out some nutritious recipes for further discussion.

4. Plan a nutritious meal and have group members prepare this. After eating the meal discuss how they found planning and preparing the meal.

Fitness

Aim: To learn about the importance of fitness to increase an overall sense of well-being.

Media: Discussion, video, exercise charts.

Activity:

1. Have a discussion on fitness – what it is, why it is important to incorporate it into a person's lifestyle. Have each group member talk about what they do to keep fit.

2. Show a video on fitness (or exercise programme) and then discuss what was shown on the video.

3. Have a discussion on personal goals of fitness. Have group members look at how fit they would like to be, what type of activity is required to achieve these goals.

4. Have a discussion on group members' interests: what are the limitations? Have each group member decide on an activity and work out a weekly schedule for them to follow.

Discharge situations

Aim: To encourage ventilation about any fears or concerns that a person might have about being discharged.

Media: index cards with possible discharge situations written on them, pens, paper, board.

Activity:

1. Have a discussion centring on feelings about leaving the institution. Ask each person how they feel about leaving: What are they looking forward to? What are they concerned about? How did they find the facility helpful? Do they know who to go to if they have any concerns? List the suggestions/items that people mention on the board.

2. Acknowledge that there are a lot of fears, anxieties or concerns about going back to the community. Have someone read out possible situations, for example:

- Your family asks what it is like being in a forensic psychiatric facility
- You overhear someone talking about crazy, mad people.
- You go for a job interview and you are asked where you have been for the last number of years.
- You meet someone you find attractive and they want to know more about you.
- You are starting to feel stressed and you don't know what to do.
- Your family expect you to do things that you don't feel comfortable about.

The group discusses the situations and suggest various ideas which are listed on the board. Look at which solutions may be more effective.

3. Acknowledge that people were having a lot of problems before they came into the facility, for example interpersonal, family, job, anger. Are those problems still there? Hand around a worksheet which states 'My problem is ....'. Each person is asked to write down one problem. Fold it over and hand it back. Then hand around a worksheet which states 'The solution is .... '. The problems are then redistributed. Each person has an attempt to work out possible solutions to the problem they have received. When everyone is finished, they take it in turns to read the problem and solution to the group. Group members are encouraged to think of additional solutions.

4. Acknowledge that goal-setting is sometimes hard to do but that it is helpful if people plan what they need to do. Discussion centres on what most needs to be done when leaving the institution, for example, finding a place to stay, transportation, etc. Hand out a work sheet entitled: 'My goal is ......'/'What I need to do is ....'. Have each person write down one goal that they see as important. Next write down the steps required to achieve that goal. Bring it back to the group for further discussion and ideas.

Social connection

Aim: To increase awareness of the individual's options for participating in enjoyable activities and in meeting new people.

Media: discussion, board, board games, guest speaker, excursion.

Activity:

1. Discuss 'how we feel about meeting people' and 'joining in social activities'. List on the board some of the issues that the group members mention, for example, don't know anyone, don't know where to go, don't know what to talk about, feel too shy and so on. Do group members have these problems in common? What have people found useful in helping them meet people and try new activities? Role-play some situations where clients meet people and make simple conversation.

2. Have group members plan a social activity, for example afternoon tea and board games. After completing the activity, discuss how people individually/personally felt about their involvement.

3. Discuss 'What enjoyable activities have we done in the past?' and 'Is that something that you would like to do in the future?'. Then go on to look at the types of community resources available – types of recreational programmes available, for example, drop-in centres, senior citizens centres, adult education. Have a guest speaker come in to talk in further depth about community resources.

4. Plan a series of outings to the community to visit recreational resources, for example, park, library, museum, club, drop-in centre, day-care programme.

Resources in the community

Aim: To acquaint group members with important community resources.

Media: map of the area, phonebook, pencils, paper, field trip, guest speakers.

Activity:

1. Invite a member of the local community centre in to discuss the role of staff at a community centre and how they can be of assistance. Look at the advantages of aftercare/follow-up programmes once people have left the institution. Have group members discuss whether or not they have been to a community centre, and how they found that experience.

2. Go on a field trip to the local community centre. Have people look up on the map where it is and work out how they are going to get there. Go to the community centre, look at the facility, meet the staff, meet some of the patients who are there attending programmes.

3. Invite a member in from the crisis team to discuss their role in acute emergency and how people can contact them. Look at the types of issues/situations that might constitute a crisis for group members. Also look at the other types of services that are available in the community such as suicide prevention, lifeline, etc.

4. Invite people in from a resource such as the local drop-in centre to discuss advantages of meeting other people and how the drop-in centre operates. Using the map work out how to get to the drop-in centre and then go on a field trip to visit the local drop-in centre.

5. Invite a member of the probation services to talk about the probation service and how the probation service can provide support and act as a liaison and a resource with other services.

SUMMARY

This chapter has looked at some of the areas that need to be addressed concerning preparing forensic psychiatric clients for the transition to the community.

REFERENCES

Anthony, W., Pierce, R., Cohen, M. *et al.* (1980) *The Skills of Rehabilitation Programing. Psychiatric Rehabilitation Practice: Series Book 2*, University Park Press, Baltimore.

Axelrod, S. and Wetzler, S. (1989) Factors associated with better compliance with psychiatric aftercare. *Hospital and Community Psychiatry*, **40**, 397–401.

Bacharach, L. (1986) Dimensions of disability. *Hospital and Community Psychiatry*, **37**, 981–2.

Champney, T. and Dzurec, L. (1992) Involvement in productive activities and satisfaction with living situations among severely mentally disabled adults. *Hospital and Community Psychiatry*, **43**, 899–903.

Choate, R., Smith, A., Cardillo, J. *et al.* (1981) Training in the use of goal attainment scaling. *Community Mental Health Journal*, **17**, 171–81.

Clary, C., Dever, A. and Schweizer, E. (1992) Psychiatric inpatients' knowledge of medication at hospital discharge. *Hospital and Community Psychiatry*, **43**, 140–4.

Cohen, M., Vitalo, R., Anthony, W. *et al.* (1980) *The Skills of Community Service Coordination. Psychiatric Rehabilitation Practice Series: Book 6*, University Park Press, Baltimore.

Drew, N. (1991) Combating the social isolation of chronic mental illness. *Journal of Psychosocial Nursing*, **29**, 15–7.

Guy, M. and Moore, L. (1982) The goal attainment scale for psychiatric inpatients. *Quality Review Bulletin*, **8**, 19–29.

Harmon, R. and Tratnack, S. (1992) Teaching hospitalized patients with serious persistent mental illness. *Journal of Psychosocial Nursing*, **30**, 33–6.

Herje, P. (1980) Hows and whys of patients contracting. *Nurse Educator*, **5**, 30–4.

Hochberger, J. and Fisher-James, L. (1992) Discharge group for chronically mentally ill. *Journal of Psychosocial Nursing*, **30**, 25–7.

Kiresuk, T. and Sherman, R. (1968) Goal attainment scaling: A general method for evaluating comprehensive community mental health programs. *Community Mental Health Journal*, **4**, 443–53.

Mohr, W. (1993) Nurse-led educational program in psychiatric settings: Developing a curriculum. *Journal of Psychosocial Nursing*, **31**, 35–8.

Peterson, C. (1986) Changing community attitudes toward the chronically mentally ill. *Hospital and Community Psychiatry*, **37**, 180–2.

Robinson, G. and Pinkney, A. (1992) Transition from the hospital to the community: Small group program. *Journal of Psychosocial Nursing*, **30**, 33–6.

Versluys, H. (1980) The remediation of role disorders through focused group work. *American Journal of Occupational Therapy*, **34**, 609–14.

Index